Reinvention

Arlene Dickinson

Reinvention

CHANGING YOUR LIFE,
YOUR CAREER, YOUR FUTURE

Collins

Reinvention
Copyright © 2019 by 761250 Alberta Ltd.
All rights reserved.

Published by Collins, an imprint of HarperCollins Publishers Ltd

First edition

HarperCollins books may be purchased for educational, business,
or sales promotional use through our Special Markets Department.

HarperCollins Publishers Ltd
Bay Adelaide Centre, East Tower
22 Adelaide Street West, 41st Floor
Toronto, Ontario, Canada
M5H 4E3

www.harpercollins.ca

Library and Archives Canada Cataloguing in Publication
information is available upon request.

ISBN 978-1-4434-5164-2

Printed and bound in the United States of America
LSC/H 9 8 7 6 5 4 3

For all the people at Venture, both past and present, and District Ventures—your talent, commitment and passion have always been key to our success, and I am better because of you.

Contents

Introduction

The night my hometown was nearly destroyed by flooding, I woke at 3 a.m. and stood watching in shock from a window thirty-odd floors above downtown Calgary. It was eerily quiet, with not a light in sight. Every tower, crane and billboard had gone dark. Buildings had been reduced to ghostly outlines. Maybe it was my imagination, but I swear that the only sound was the faint rushing of water spilling over the edges of the Bow River. My heart raced.

I was witnessing one of the worst natural disasters in Canada's history. In the summer of 2013, heavy rainfall triggered unprecedented flooding in Alberta, leading to mandatory evacuations throughout the southern part of the province. But like a lot of people, I'd rolled my eyes when the mayor of Calgary issued a warning not to go downtown for any reason. Westerners tend to think of themselves as tough and resourceful, able to deal with just about anything life throws at them, and I'm no different. So I didn't evacuate, though I did take the precaution of seeking higher ground: I went to stay with a friend who lives in a high-rise, grumbling all the while about the inconvenience.

So why were we still up there when the river surged into the city, watching this catastrophe unfold? Denial. Neither of us could believe it was really happening. It felt like a horror movie, one with a huge special effects budget.

When I woke up for real at 6 a.m., Calgary was a watery ghost town. I could barely make sense of what I was seeing. A car floated along in the water swirling through the downtown streets, bobbing like a bath toy. Helicopters whirred overhead. My city was drowning.

Five people had lost their lives, many thousands had been displaced, and the financial toll was in the billions. People had seen their homes and livelihoods washed away overnight, in a torrent of muddy water. I was relatively lucky—blessed, actually, because my family and friends were all safe, thank God. But the flood left Venture, the marketing company I had spent twenty-five years building, in ruins.

No one, least of all me, had expected this; our offices were outside the downtown core, far from the surging Bow. But the day before the flood, the police had knocked on every door, including ours, telling people to get out while they still could. I couldn't believe it. We were in the midst of several big pitches—this abundance of caution would cost us a full day of work. Our IT guy had the wherewithal to grab Venture's backup servers before locking up the old schoolhouse we'd so lovingly restored and converted into our headquarters, and everyone went home, fully expecting to come to work as usual the next day. That night, however, water rushed into the historic building, flooding the basement offices. As we discovered later, it rose nearly to the ceiling, covering all but the topmost step of the staircase up to the first floor. Computers, desks, files, office supplies, the espresso machine in the staff kitchen, irreplaceable hard copies of our early work—all were submerged.

Finally, after days of heroic rescue efforts by responders, the flood water receded. Most people were allowed to return to their homes (if they were still standing), yet police told us that Venture was still off limits. A combination of half-drained water and downed electrical wires made it too dangerous to enter the building. But I needed to see for myself. I drove through the broken city, weaving between vacuum trucks and emergency vehicles, and gingerly pushed the door open. A coating of thick brown sludge, muddy silt from the river, covered every surface. There was a sickeningly sour smell in the air, like rotting food. Flood water is contaminated with all kinds of gross bacteria; we would have to get rid of everything, even furniture and supplies that hadn't got wet. To this day, when I look at insurance photos of the devastation, I seize up inside.

The months that followed were chaotic and depressing. Marketing is a service business, and our clients, many of whom weren't located in Calgary, still expected us to do the work we'd been hired to do, on the timelines we'd promised—a reasonable expectation. But the team was under incredible emotional stress. Some people's cars and homes had been destroyed, and they were camping out with friends and family, living out of suitcases. Even those who hadn't experienced personal losses were reeling; witnessing destruction on such a massive scale is traumatic.

I was reeling too. I'd skated past trouble so many times in the previous twenty-five years that I'd been lulled into a false sense of security. Without even recognizing it was happening, I'd come to believe that my business was untouchable and my professional judgment infallible. I'd seen it all, done it all. What could possibly go wrong? I now had the answer to that question: everything.

The logistical challenges alone were mind-boggling. I was running around dealing with insurance companies, attempting to clean up the mess in our old office and trying to find a new one. So many Calgary businesses were in the same predicament that the temporary space we were lucky enough to find was already crammed with refugee staff from other displaced companies. Still, we tried to forge ahead with our usual can-do work ethic: business as usual. As fate would have it, we had four reviews scheduled with existing clients, to determine whether they'd renew their contracts with us or go with other agencies; these are all-out pitches, where you remind clients of the heights you've scaled together and then present a plan for an even rosier future. But our team was scattered across the city, with some people working from home while others were distributed among three different rental offices, all in different locations. Collaboration was extraordinarily difficult, and the quality of the work we were putting out was severely compromised.

We lost all four clients. One of the CEOs told me, "We wanted Venture to win, we really did. But it was as though a whole different agency showed up to pitch." He was right. We were limping along, just trying to get through another day, not to excel. We didn't sign a single new client during that time, which was very unusual.

In a state of grief and uncertainty, many people quit, and since we weren't generating new work, I had to lay others off. Soon, half my business and half my team had vanished. Those who remained were anxious, understandably, so I was trying to project calm and certainty, but inside I was starting to panic. I was plowing my own money into the business to keep the lights on, but the bank was telling me it was a lost cause. *Pull the plug, Arlene. Venture has had a good run, but it's over.*

My lowest point came when the chief marketing officer of a company we'd done business with for many years called me into her office and told me that since the company's focus had shifted to the American market, she'd decided to hire a marketing firm in the US. Years before, when we'd landed this client, it had been a coup, one that gave us clout and credibility in the marketplace. The company hadn't been one of our larger accounts for quite a while, so the loss was more symbolic than anything else, but what it symbolized to me was that Venture was in irreversible decline. I did something I've never done before in a professional situation, and something I've explicitly told others not to do, because it reveals such a lack of self-control. I broke down and began crying—not a discreet tear or two, which would have been completely fine, but wrenching sobs that simply wouldn't stop. I managed to gasp out that I was truly grateful to have had the company as a client and was very proud of the work we'd done together, but accepted and respected their decision, and wished them the best of luck. Yet I could not stop weeping. It was mortifying. The CMO was a smart, tough businesswoman, someone I really respected; I think she'd seen me the same way, and didn't quite know what to make of the fact that I was having a breakdown in her office. I tried to explain that the flood seemed to have washed away everything I'd worked so hard to build, but I was probably crying too hard to be coherent. Eventually she left me alone in her office with a box of Kleenex so I could try to pull myself together.

When I finally stumbled out of there, eyes bloodshot and heart close to broken, part of me wanted to head straight to my lawyer's office to start the process of winding down my company. I felt both hopeless and humiliated. I was very fortunate in that Venture had long since ceased being my main source of income; my interests were spread across many different businesses and investments, so I'd be okay financially. It would be easy to shutter the company, I told myself.

But no sooner had I allowed myself to entertain the thought than something in me balked. *No.* I could not do that to my team. Or to myself. Giving up on the company would be like giving up on myself. Until that moment, I hadn't fully comprehended that Venture was really where my heart and soul resided. I'd built it with my own hands, starting there as a single mom who could fit everything she knew about advertising on the head of a pin and still have room for the Lord's Prayer. Within ten years of joining the agency, I'd managed to buy out my partners and become the 100 percent owner. In turn, Venture had launched me into many other successes, lending me credibility for *Dragons' Den* and creating exciting new investment opportunities.

Very few independent marketing firms last more than ten years; they're swallowed up by larger firms or they fail, because it's a tough business, and one where the flashy new kid on the block has an advantage. But we'd survived for a quarter of a century. For the first time, I realized how central our longevity was to my sense of self-worth. I also realized that, distracted by all the other irons I had in the fire, I'd become complacent about Venture. The fact that I had taken my legacy business for granted—the one that had not only created a platform for me but still provided a livelihood for many other people—made it all the more devastating to think that I was on the cusp of losing it.

I've experienced tough times, even depression, in my life. Mostly, I've been able to compartmentalize and manage through the low moments. But there was no compartment big enough to contain these overwhelming feelings of loss, fear, shame and guilt. They spilled over, just as the river had, swamping every waking moment.

At night, instead of sleeping, I'd compile mental lists of all the things that had gone wrong. We should have started preparing for those agency reviews much earlier. We should have moved our vital records and equipment up from the basement at the first mention of a flood—why had they been stored down there anyway? The company should have been strong enough to withstand a slump. I hadn't reacted quickly enough, or in the right way, to the disaster. And I couldn't stop thinking about all the people who'd helped build Venture but were now pounding the pavement, looking for jobs.

The list of ways I'd screwed up and been screwed over by the flood grew and grew until the weight of it immobilized me. Literally. I could not move my body to get out of bed. It was as if a dark cloud had filled my head. I could only think one thing: *I don't want to do this anymore.* I wasn't contemplating suicide, but I couldn't see a way out of the feeling. I couldn't even open the blinds, as if the sunlight would melt away what was left of me.

Staring at the ceiling and feeling as terrible as I've ever felt in my life, I suddenly had a flashback to the weeks after my first divorce, when I'd spent whole days lying on my dad's couch, weeping. The judge had told me I had no hope of getting custody of my kids unless I could provide for them. I couldn't imagine how, armed only with a high school diploma, I could possibly get a good-enough job to do that. Cue more weeping. "Well, who do you think is going to fix this, Arlene?" my dad finally said. "You?" I said hopefully, through tears. "No," he replied gently, "you are. You are going to get up off this couch and get yourself a job. You have it in you to save yourself. It's time to get started."

Up until that point, I'd relied on the Mormon Church for my sense of direction. Being a good wife and good mother was supposed to deliver all the fulfillment I required. Well, for me, it hadn't been enough. But it had never occurred to me that it was therefore my responsibility to try to figure out what would be enough. Instead, I'd acted out my longing for emotional sustenance by having an affair—triggering the implosion of my marriage, the loss of my children and my expulsion from the faith.

I had no choice but to find a new sense of direction. Lying on my dad's couch, clinging to the idea that I was a victim—of my church, or a loveless marriage, or a heartless judge—wasn't helping me do that. In fact, it was making me feel helpless to improve my life. In the most diplomatic way possible, my father suggested that perhaps the story I was telling myself wasn't wholly accurate. Maybe I'd played a larger role in my own sorry spiral than I cared to admit.

One good thing about hitting rock bottom: you're truly open to considering every possibility. Though it hurt to admit it, the hard truth was that the road to that couch had been paved with some really bad choices. Mine. I'd married very young, against my parents' advice and long before I knew my own heart and mind. I hadn't attended university, though my parents and teachers had urged me to apply. And then there was the affair, a spectacularly bad choice that couldn't possibly be pinned on anyone else.

Surprisingly, cataloguing all these mistakes did not make me feel worse. Sobering as it was to accept responsibility for the consequences of my own decisions, it was freeing too. Clearly, I *was* in charge of my own destiny to a large degree—which meant that maybe, just maybe, I could change course and head in a better direction. One thing was certain: my father was right. No one else could fix the mess I was in and reinvent my life. I was my only hope.

Thinking about all this as I lay in bed post-flood, the parallels were obvious. Just as weeping on my dad's couch had achieved nothing, nor would cursing the flood and feeling sorry for myself. Persuading myself that I was a victim of circumstance only made me feel powerless; taking responsibility for my choices, especially the worst ones, empowered me to make better ones.

As I rewound the tape of my life again and again to that moment when I finally got up off my dad's couch and began to change my life, six words came to me: *we need to reinvent the company*. It sounds corny, but if you've ever had an epiphany, you know what I'm talking about. It really was as though a light bulb appeared over my head, with the words inscribed in one of those cartoon clouds. And I knew instantly that they were the right words. I wasn't sure which direction we needed to head, or how we'd pull it off, only that we had to try to change course. Immediately.

Evolution is the key to survival

Sometimes it's unmistakable that a company is at a crossroads. There's a scandal, or sales are tanking, or a disruptive new start-up is fundamentally changing the industry. Or maybe the sweet smell of opportunity is in the air: a major expansion is under way, or a new product is ready to launch. Either way, it's clear that big changes are inevitable, and they will determine the company's future.

More often, though, a business idles at a crucial intersection without recognizing it. Threats are minimized or ignored—and so are opportunities. That was the situation with Venture, pre-flood. Everything seemed to be humming along smoothly. Sure, we were always looking to do better and to expand the business. But I was also looking to avoid risk. And changing the business in significant ways, even to take advantage of great opportunities, would entail significant risk: we might lose clients, lose money, lose traction, lose staff. Of course, all of those things I'd tried to avoid happened anyway. Risk aversion not only backfired but led to the far more serious risk that the company might be wiped out entirely.

Here's the truly embarrassing part: I should have known better. Even the most junior marketer knows that companies that don't evolve can't survive. In fact, marketing is all about helping companies evolve, though it may not seem that way at first glance.

On the surface, the job of a marketer is just to help businesses position their products so that people want to buy more of them, either by creating a brand identity from scratch or by repositioning an existing brand, and then figuring out how to communicate that identity to the masses. What makes it tricky is that you can't just concoct a nice story and tell it in some flashy ads (unless you want to destroy your own credibility, along with your client's). Ultimately, a brand is the sum total of people's experience with a product over time—how well it works, what it looks like, what it costs and where it's sold, whether they used it growing up, whether they trust it, and so on—so they know very well when you're not telling the truth.

What a company actually *does*, versus what it says it's doing in an ad, matters. If your ads say that your cookies are wholesome but in fact they're stuffed with carcinogenic chemicals, people notice. No matter how heartwarming your ads are, your brand won't be viewed as "wholesome" but as "harmful." Broader cultural changes also affect brands. Twenty years ago, what mattered most about cookie packaging was that it caught your eye and kept the cookies fresh. Today, being environmentally conscious is important, so if you want to be known as wholesome, your packaging had better be sourced from sustainable materials and be recyclable. And let's not forget the way the company is run. If your CEO is revealed to have harassed an employee, or shown up at a Halloween party in blackface, or cracked homophobic jokes, your cookies and packaging could be the most wholesome in the world, but your brand won't be "wholesome." It will be "disgusting."

Creating or transforming a brand, then, isn't about manipulating public perception by coming up with cool ads. It's about helping companies evolve and reinvent themselves so that absolutely everything about them, from the logo on their products to the way the CEO handles customers' complaints, sends the same consistent message—and then coming up with cool ads that trumpet that message.

Helping companies reinvent themselves in this way was our bread and butter at Venture.

Ironically, though, we'd been standing still. Just as the cobbler's children don't have shoes, our own company had not been evolving.

Reinvention is methodical

I used to be amazed when the management teams of distressed businesses would come to us looking for help with problems that had clearly been brewing for years. *Why did they wait so long? There were so many warning signs along the way.* Well, I understand it better now. You're so focused on putting out daily fires that the big red Danger! signs on the horizon barely register. Until we were right at the edge of the cliff, staring into the abyss, I hadn't even been fully aware how much the landscape around us had changed. Hip boutique agencies with a fresh approach had sprung up all over the place; Venture was old news. At the same time, the business itself had changed, with a far greater emphasis on data, analytics and digital marketing than ever before. And a lot of the traditional functions of marketing agencies—creating logos, buying media— were being commoditized, so it was possible to source them online without ever setting foot in a marketing agency. To stay in the game, we should already have reinvented ourselves.

And there was something else: I had changed too. I thought of myself as an entrepreneur, but I wasn't behaving like one— pushing the envelope, trying to do new things in a new way, questioning the status quo. I had *become* the status quo.

On some level, I was aware of the contradiction but not sure what to do about it. Mostly, I just felt restless at Venture. *Now what?* I'd find myself wondering, as I looked around the bustling office. *Is this all there is?* Everything seemed to be going along just fine without me, so I flipped the autopilot switch and checked out, to focus on the new world of mentoring entrepreneurs and investing in early-stage companies that I'd discovered through *Dragons' Den*. I didn't ask myself why I'd disconnected emotionally from my company, much less what I could do about it. All I knew was that I felt a whole lot more engaged when helping young companies get off the ground than I did when developing marketing plans for corporate Canada. But I'd never seriously considered reshaping Venture so that it better reflected my interests. That would require energy—a lot of energy. And I'd already spread myself so thin that, like a hamster on a wheel, I was in perpetual motion, going so fast that I barely noticed the company wasn't moving forward too.

In a sense, then, the flood saved us. Without it, we probably would have continued bumping along on cruise control, oblivious of the threats to our existence, until it was too late to do anything about them. It's happened to much larger companies than ours (just ask anyone who used to work at Blockbuster). But because I was forced to take stock, I recognized, just in time, that the flood hadn't jeopardized the company. I had. While I'd been confidently telling others how to overhaul their businesses, I hadn't been minding my own.

There was, however, one silver lining. A pretty big one: I did know how to reinvent a company—someone else's company, anyway. Reinvention wasn't a threatening or mysterious concept to me, the way it is to some business owners. Sometimes, the management team of a company strenuously resists change; they want to keep doing things the way they always have, only with better ads. Other times, they're so desperate to turn things around that they'd happily chuck everything—logo, media strategy, website, the works—on the spot. But when the goal is lasting transformation, neither stubborn resistance nor a frenzy of willy-nilly changes will do the trick.

Reinvention is a methodical, analytical process with discrete steps and predictable stages. It's not flat-out creation: you have to work with what you already have, tweaking and repurposing and redirecting as needed. You're renovating, not building a whole new house. The process takes longer than you'd like, always, and success is never guaranteed, but it isn't some crazy crapshoot either. Whether you are able to pull off a reinvention depends to a very large extent on your insight into your company's strengths and weaknesses, your understanding of the market opportunities, and the depth of your own commitment to trust your findings, even if they're not to your liking, and execute your strategy.

I embarked on the reinvention of Venture, then, with a clear idea of how to proceed and no illusions that it would be painless. And it wasn't. I'd weathered a lot of storms in my life, but this was a tsunami. The lows were the lowest I've ever experienced (and that's saying something). I had moments very close to despair, when I distrusted my own instincts and judgment, and kept going only because I'd told my team I would not give up. Quite apart from the emotional toll of executing a 180-degree turn, it's mentally and physically gruelling. I probably aged ten years in two and a half, from sheer stress.

Later on, I'll explain in detail how we did it, but for now, let's fast-forward to the happy ending. Actually, it's more of a beginning, because Venture is no longer a traditional marketing agency. It's a very different company, with a newly minted mission and a new client base, and one that's dramatically stronger and more successful than at any point in our history.

The beauty of a plan

I am different too. I've never been happier or felt more engaged in life and excited about the future. I can't pretend that this was all part of my grand plan, though; my own reinvention was a totally unexpected benefit of reinventing Venture. In order to save the company, I had to think hard about why it was worth saving in the first place. What was our purpose, anyway? That question led directly to another one: what was *my* purpose in life? As with many entrepreneurs, my identity is entwined with my company's. Venture is, in a very real way, an expression of my own interests and values; in turn, I'm influenced by the work we do. Inevitably, then, as we went back to the drawing board to try to envision a post-flood future, I was thinking about what kind of future I wanted too. In other words, I began applying the same process, the one we'd always used to help other businesses reinvent, to my own personal life. And lo and behold, it worked.

When I first realized that a process that helps businesses could also help me, as a person, it was one of those "aha!" moments that changes everything. Suddenly, everything that I'd been doing in my professional life up to that point made sense: I'd been practising. Every time I'd walked a client through a brand reinvention, I'd been learning how to do it for myself. I was getting ready for a time when I'd really need this knowledge. At fifty-seven, it had arrived. I needed to call on everything I'd learned about turning companies around to turn my own life around.

I don't want to sound glib about it, because changing your life is never easy. But this time around, it was definitely easier and far less emotionally turbulent than it was when I reinvented myself post-divorce. The difference wasn't that I was more mature or had less at stake; in some ways, the risks were greater, and I had even more to lose. The difference was that I had a strong conceptual framework for thinking about where I wanted to go and how to get there, and a clear set of practical steps to follow, which kept me on track and focused, especially when my emotions threatened to derail me.

Like a lot of people, I'd been dissatisfied with certain aspects of my life for a while, but I hadn't done anything about it. Just as I'd taken my company for granted and grown complacent, I'd grown complacent about my own life too. Sure, I wanted to change, and fully intended to do so. Someday. There's always a good reason to postpone any kind of upheaval, and one of the best is uncertainty: about your ultimate destination, whether you have what it takes to get there, and what you'll have to give up to do it. Having a road map to follow stripped away those excuses and helped me get rid of the emotional baggage—fear, self-doubt—that had been weighing me down and holding me back. I was finally able to get going, and as soon as I did, my first thought was, *Why didn't I do this years ago?*

There is nothing—nothing!—more powerful, more fulfilling and more liberating than taking control of your own destiny and creating a better life for yourself. But you can't simply wish it into existence, as some self-help gurus advise, or pray for it to happen. You need more than inspiration, cheerleading and snappy slogans. Whether you have a specific goal, or just the vaguest sense of the kind of life you'd like to have, you need practical, actionable advice. An actual plan. And that's what you'll find on the following pages.

Full disclosure: you won't find miracle cures, magic tricks or shortcuts. Reinvention is hard work, and no one else can do it for you. But what I can do is show you how to narrow in on what marketers call your brand identity (which is really just who you are at your core); how to use that information to gauge your prospects and determine what opportunities are realistic and achievable; how to create a strategy to achieve your goals; and how to communicate all of this to others (spoiler alert: some people are not going to be thrilled that you're changing your life).

It's the tried-and-true process I've used for three decades with companies that want to establish or transform their brands, and which, almost by accident, I discovered could also be used to transform a life: mine. And yours.

A goal or a dream is not enough

The world is changing faster than at any time in the course of human history. Most of us feel this in our bones and know intuitively that to keep up, we have to evolve. But given the pace of change, evolution may seem hopeless. *What's the point? There's no way to get ahead of the curve.* You just got used to Facebook but now it's Instagram, and tomorrow it will be something some visionary kid is cooking up in his parents' garage right this minute. Jobs are being automated out of existence, and headlines warn that artificial intelligence will put millions more people out of work. Then there's the political upheaval around the world, the upending of the global economic order, shifting gender norms and sexual politics. Some of this change is urgent and welcome. Some of it feels scary and apocalyptic. All put together, it can feel completely overwhelming, both for businesses and for individuals. The temptation might be to stand still, braced for disaster, like someone waiting out an earthquake in a door frame.

But you can't stop the clock. And unless you're already leading your ideal life, standing still is not a great option. Most people can think of a few big changes they'd like to make in the time they have left on earth. Maybe you don't love your job, or even like it much. Maybe you've been thinking about going back to school, or switching industries, or moving to a new city or country, or starting a family, or starting a business, or leaving an unhappy relationship, or radically changing your lifestyle, or finally doing something about that dream that's been simmering on the back burner for, well, forever. Or maybe big changes are coming whether you like it or not: you've lost your job or your relationship, or had a health scare, or suddenly you have an empty nest and no clue how to fill your days.

Whatever the case, having a step-by-step plan for reinvention can mean the difference between wanting or needing to change your life and actually doing it. Having a goal or a dream of a better life is not enough. Just think of all the people you know who dream (or, more likely, dreamed) of being singers, or actors, or athletes, or artists, or business tycoons, or prime minister. Some of them may even have pursued their dreams with considerable courage and tenacity, but if there's a mismatch between the dream and the skill set, or a mismatch between the skill set and what the market actually values, perseverance doesn't matter.

It might even be a negative, as we see all the time on *Dragons' Den*. Entrepreneurs come on the show and proudly announce that they're drowning in debt to keep their companies afloat, despite never selling a single widget, because "you never give up on a dream." Well, you should, if that dream has turned your life into a nightmare. And then you should look for another dream, one that's achievable.

But many people are so swept up in their own emotional investment in a dream that they can't think clearly about whether it's realistic, much less how to go about achieving it. This is where a business framework is incredibly helpful. It removes emotion from the proceedings, replacing it with hefty doses of logic and realism, and makes it easier to determine the difference between a dream worth pursuing and a never-going-to-happen fantasy. That distinction is clear in business, because emotion doesn't cloud the issue and you can focus-group and market-test ideas to figure out which ones are winners. If a gluten-free pasta manufacturer came to me wanting help to morph into a shoe company, it would be glaringly obvious, after step one of our process, that the goal simply was not achievable, or even desirable. But by step two or three, another goal—manufacturing and distributing healthy meals to schools, say—would probably have emerged.

Which brings me to a very important point: you have to work with what you have. Reinvention doesn't mean scrapping everything you are and starting all over again. You still have the same core values, beliefs and capabilities you did before (whether you were aware you had them or not). You're not enrolling in the witness protection program and getting a whole new identity. You're still *you*.

Reinvention is about recycling and renewing your talents and interests and using them in a different way. You don't have to—nor should you—erase your past and morph into a whole new person. You can reshape your life in ways that make you feel a whole lot happier and more fulfilled simply by figuring out how to capitalize on who you already are, and then coming up with a strategy to push yourself to new heights.

But let's be clear: "You can be anyone, you can do anything!" is—sorry—a lie. It's also a recipe for disappointment, inaction and low self-esteem. You can't do anything, any more than I can (or ever could have) become an Olympic track star or a supermodel.

Again, you have to work with what you have. And your reinvention, like mine, may take you to a somewhat different destination than you've been dreaming of or hoping to reach. But it will take you somewhere, because while you can't do *anything*, you can do *something*. Something that makes you excited to get out of bed in the morning. Something that makes you feel you are being true to your best self. Something that changes your life for the better.

More good news: reinvention doesn't require Herculean inner strength, incredible luck, family money or divine intervention. It's not rocket science, and you don't need specialized training or a fancy degree to pull it off. What you do need is courage, conviction and a practical game plan, which you happen to be holding in your hand right now. Even if that's all you've got, don't worry—working on the other two is all part of the plan.

Let's get started.

Part One

GETTING STARTED

So you want to make a change. You have your eye on a new job. You dream of taking your love of travel and building a life on another continent. Maybe you know you should leave a relationship that's not working. Maybe you want to start a small business, or go back to school.

But then . . . nothing. Change never comes.

As with companies, so with people: many of us cling to the safety of the known, even when we aren't particularly happy or don't feel we're achieving all we could, until we're absolutely forced to change direction—as I was, by the flood. Afterwards, like me, you find yourself wondering why you didn't make a move earlier. Sure, changing your life is difficult. But it's rarely as difficult as you built it up to be beforehand.

You've probably experienced this phenomenon in miniature if you've ever managed to quit smoking or drinking, start a new exercise routine or begin eating healthily. Once you finally get started, the going is never as tough as you thought it would be, partly because you start experiencing rewards immediately. I don't mean that you become a paragon of good health overnight, but you do start feeling better about yourself pretty much instantly. You feel stronger and more in control—and you stop judging yourself so harshly. *There, I finally did something!* Sometimes something as minor as a new haircut can feel liberating, not because you suddenly look like you stepped off the cover of *Vogue*, but because it helps you see yourself in a slightly different light. The fact that even small changes are so rewarding speaks to the promise of wholesale transformation.

But here's the thing: sometimes the universe doesn't deliver the push you need to get going on a full-scale reinvention. There is no flood, no disaster—nor a brass ring dangling within arm's reach, practically begging you to try to grab it. And if fate doesn't force your hand, you may well stay stuck.

If you're in your twenties or thirties, you might be thinking, "Well, that will never happen to me. I'd never let it happen! Plus, I still have plenty of time to take my shot." But it's astonishing how many smart, sensible people wake up in mid-life and realize they're on a path that just feels . . . wrong. Maybe someone else—a parent, friend, mentor, spouse—thought it was a good idea. Or maybe they chose the path themselves, but it's not taking them where they thought it would. Regardless, at the very moment in life when they should be flying high, they feel as though they never even got off the runway. This is the juncture where someone may wind up becoming a mid-life cliché—buying a sports car, or having an affair, or getting a facelift (or all three). Aging gracefully is difficult when you feel you missed out on the life you were supposed to have but, instead of moving on, you try to turn back time.

It's just not possible. Once some doors in life close, they never reopen. While a second (or third, or fourth) chance at happiness is yours for the taking, it's almost guaranteed that you won't get a second chance to, say, go to Harvard or become a rock star or travel the world with Cirque du Soleil. Some dreams and goals have expiration dates, and they're always sooner than you think.

So the question to ask yourself right now, especially if you have a specific goal or dream but haven't done much about it, is how you'd feel five, ten or twenty years from now if you'd never tried to achieve it. Let's say you stayed on the course you're on right now and didn't even attempt to change direction. Would you wind up looking wistfully in the rear-view mirror, sighing, "Oh, if only I'd done _____. Why didn't I?" If so, you have all the information you need to get started on the first task of reinvention: persuading yourself that you can't wait any longer.

Chapter 1

Excuses, excuses

Not all that long ago, an Albertan entrepreneur came to Venture looking for help marketing a terrific product that had the potential to break out nationally, maybe even internationally. People in the office were jockeying to work on the account—the product was that good. We researched the market extensively, came up with ideas about how to brand the product, connected the CEO with retailers and distributors who could get it into stores across the country, and unveiled a marketing and communications strategy. And the CEO loved everything about the work we'd done, except for one thing: implementing the strategy would require a significant investment of money and energy. Well, yes. Reinventing a mom-and-pop local business as a national brand does cost something—but consider the potential rewards! Wasn't that the whole reason the CEO had come to us in the first place, to try to take the company to the next level?

The dream of building a powerhouse brand was achievable; we had the market research to prove it. But when the moment of truth arrived, the CEO's confidence evaporated, replaced by a severe case of cold feet. The plan was so ambitious. More people would have to be hired. Production would have to be stepped up. Maybe we could cut out the social media piece, or do it on the cheap? And what about the website—was a top-notch site really necessary? And so on. The CEO had a lot of good excuses for not following through on the reinvention strategy, which is why, unless you live in Calgary, you've never heard of this product. The company is still struggling along, trying to implement bits and pieces of our plan on its own, without much success. Business reinvention requires a comprehensive approach, one fuelled not only by cash but by conviction.

There were some long faces around our office when we finally realized that this company, which we'd all thought of as the little engine that could, wasn't going to be reinvented as a booming national business. Despite having a great product. Despite research, statistics and charts galore demonstrating the existence of a large potential market. Despite having a brand strategy all teed up and ready to go. It was the little engine that could, all right . . . but had decided not to.

Disheartening as it is when a CEO turns his or her back on a company's potential, it's just a company. If it limps along or even fails outright, it's not the end of the world. Employees disperse and find other jobs. Customers find another way to get a similar product or service. Another company usually comes along to take over the premises and buy the manufacturing equipment. Even a founder who's forced to declare bankruptcy can rise from the ashes and build something amazing.

This is one big difference between reinventing a company and reinventing your own life: you may not get a second chance. You only have one life, and some windows of opportunity open briefly then close forever.

Here's the other big difference: if you need to, or want to, reinvent but don't even try, that really *is* the end of a world—your world, the one you might have created for yourself. And that isn't just disappointing. It's tragic (and that's a word I don't use lightly).

So before we move on to the process of identifying your core purpose and currency—all the things that make you *you*, and which should guide your reinvention—we need to take a brief time out to tour the biggest obstacles in your path. I'm talking about the ones you may be wheeling into place at this very moment: your excuses for avoiding change.

Many people, like the CEO I just told you about, fervently embrace the promise of self-improvement . . . right until the moment they are required to take action. Then their internal critic slams on the brakes. We all have one: that little voice that whispers discouragement and reinforces self-doubt at crucial moments. It can sound extremely persuasive and rational in your own head, so you need to know how to argue with it and shut it down in order to keep moving forward. This is one debate you absolutely need to win.

"I'm too busy looking after everyone else"

I spent the first part of my life shaping myself according to what I thought other people wanted. By the time I was twenty-one years old, I was a good wife, a good mother and the perfect Mormon churchgoer. A classic pleaser, in other words, trying to be all things to all people, and trying to please everyone but myself.

Suppressing your own needs and living for others is exhausting; pleasers experience measurably higher stress levels, which can cause sleeplessness, anxiety and depression.

It's also an excellent way to ensure you stay frozen in place, for two reasons. First, changing your life in fundamental ways takes time and energy; you don't have much of either when your focus is figuring out what other people want, then supplying it. Second, if you're running around trying to keep other people happy, they won't want you to stop. They've got it good! If you try to back off on the pleasing, there will be loud grumbling, if not a protest march—and the mere idea of upsetting someone else strikes terror into the heart of the average pleaser.

So one of the most important questions to ask yourself before you start figuring out how to reinvent your life is "Who am I living for?" Are you the person who, when called on to come into the office for the third Sunday in a row, will do it even though you're busy or tired, or just don't feel like it, because the idea of letting other people down makes you feel too guilty? Are you the go-to emotional caretaker for everyone you know? Are you doing the vast majority of the work at home, despite the presence of an able-bodied spouse and children who are fully capable of dish washing and dog walking? If you're nodding (or wincing) in recognition, you have your answer. You're living for other people.

Now, there's nothing wrong with that so long as you truly feel fulfilled. But if, deep inside, there's something you still want to do—*need* to do, in order to feel whole—and yet you haven't made any progress, you have a real problem, just as I did in my twenties. Living for other people makes it difficult, if not impossible, to live for yourself. *But I have no other choice!* you may be thinking. *No one else in the office will do the grunt work to get this report out the door.*

Plus, my husband's mom is ill, my kids have hockey practice or tutoring every day after school, and I'm hosting my friend's baby shower next week. You're saying I should just turn my back on my commitments?!

No. But there's a difference between having legitimate obligations and simply being unwilling to say no. Some people take on too much because they have difficulty asserting themselves; others do it because they like to feel indispensable. And, perhaps unconsciously, some people look after everyone else because it makes it very easy to procrastinate about making changes in their own lives.

I know it can feel impossible to scale back when a lot of other people are counting on you. But bear this in mind: if you collapsed from nervous exhaustion tomorrow and the doctor put you on two weeks' bedrest effective immediately, everyone would somehow muddle through. You're not as indispensable as you might think— except to your own reinvention. Without you, it's never going to happen. You are the only person who can change your own life. *You* need to be able to count on you too.

So here's the very first change to make if you're serious about charting a new course for yourself: you need to break the yes-habit and start saying no. Whether it's an invitation to serve on a community board or a request to volunteer at your kids' school, if you can't afford the time, say no. Politely but firmly, without a lot of explanations or excuses that invite someone else to keep begging (or guilting) you to change your mind. Ditto for lunch with the friend you're no longer even sure you like all that much. And after-work drinks with the gossipy co-worker you don't entirely trust. You need to reclaim as much of your own time as possible.

Another way to do that is to accept help when it's offered. If friends or family remark that you seem overwhelmed and ask if there's anything they can do to help, say, "Why, yes!" And then ask them to take on a specific, time-limited task, like driving one of the kids to soccer practice or dropping off that huge sack of outgrown clothing at Goodwill. A lot of people are happy to lend a helping hand, so long as you're not asking them to assemble Ikea furniture or look after your cat for a week.

Also, you should ask for help if it's not being offered. If, for instance, you're doing most of the janitorial work at home, invest a little time in training everyone else to pick up the slack. Even very little kids can help fold laundry, set and clear the table, and pick up their own stuff (when older kids object, show them some of the research that proves that kids with chores do better in all areas of their lives). Some of the time and energy you're expending on others must be redirected to meeting your own needs, starting with figuring out what they are (more on this very soon).

In order to do that, you'll need to separate yourself from other people's demands and needs—and perceptions. It's hard to figure out who you really are and what you really want when you're accustomed to seeing the world, and yourself, through the eyes of family, friends and co-workers. You may be overly invested in how they see you, too. *Everyone thinks I'm really nice. I don't want them to think I'm the pushy, ambitious type.*

Whenever I hear a woman—and it's always a woman—say something along those lines, I am trying to train myself to point out, as gently as possible, that ambition is not a dirty word. Ambition doesn't make you less feminine, less empathetic, less nice or less nurturing. Ambition doesn't make you less of anything, actually, and it is absolutely crucial if you want to make more of yourself. If there are people in your life who make you feel that it's wrong to want to be the best you can be, the problem is theirs, not yours. Speaking of obligations, here's one: you have an obligation to yourself to reach your potential and achieve your goals.

The bottom line is this: to change your life, you have to be comfortable being the star of your own movie. I've struggled with this, as many women of my generation have. We were conditioned to play the perpetual supporting role, serving a man's needs above all and carefully designing our own decisions in ways that would prop him up. To younger women, raised with a completely different sense of their own possibilities, this probably sounds hilariously retro. It does to me now, too. But I've been in a few of those old-school relationships—ones where everything I did was to make my partner happy, because if he wasn't happy, nobody was happy. There was no room for me to be myself, no air to breathe and certainly no space for me to reinvent myself.

This is the real danger of living for other people: it means that no one is living for you. And you are the only person in the world who can do anything about that.

"I'm too scared"

I have a friend who says that she spent the last sixteen years of her eighteen-year marriage trying to convince herself to leave. Although she was married, she felt like a single mom. Between travel for work, entertaining clients and nights out with his friends, her husband was absent far more often than he was home. When he was home, he was usually glued to his phone, and would shoo her and their kids away if they "disturbed" him. Emotionally, the couple's connection was almost non-existent. "One year, I counted up the number of times we'd done something together, even watching TV, just the two of us. It was twice," she remembers. Still, lonely and unhappy as she was, she stayed. "I was scared I'd be alone for the rest of my life, scared that I couldn't support our kids, scared that it would scar them for life if I got divorced," she says in a wondering voice, as though speaking about a person she barely recognizes.

Then, one fine day, her husband came home and announced, out of the blue, that he'd lost his job. And oh, by the way, they needed to sell the house. Immediately. He'd managed their finances, because she "didn't have a good head for numbers"; two years earlier, he'd forged her signature to remortgage their home, and had invested the money, along with their savings, in a friend's surefire business idea. Sure enough, it had failed. Everything was gone. Including her reluctance to act: within a week, she'd filed for divorce.

The next few years were not easy, to say the least, but finally, at forty-eight, her career started to take off. "I threw myself into it," she explains, "because I had no other choice. I was broke, and I had two kids who needed everything that kids need. But also, I got a *lot* better at my job. I became more focused, to the point where I could do the same amount of work in half the time, or even less." Why? Well, being happier meant she had more energy, and she freed up a lot of mental real estate once she stopped debating with herself about whether or not to leave her marriage. After she'd reinvented herself as a successful professional, she had the confidence to start dating again and, in her early fifties, remarried. Happily this time.

"I kick myself that I spent so many years being miserable, as though I was powerless to do anything about it," she says now. "Looking back, my fears were misplaced. I *could* support my kids, and the split actually wound up improving their relationship with their dad—he spent a lot more time with them than he had when we were married. And I didn't wind up alone. But even if my worst fears had come to pass, they were so minor compared to what I sacrificed in the meantime. I frittered away sixteen years of my life, both professionally and personally. Sure, I had friends, and interests, and a great connection with my kids, but I achieved so much less and felt so much worse about myself than I could have."

She'll never get those years back. Nevertheless, she considers herself lucky. If her husband hadn't squandered their savings, she would probably still be with him, squandering her life. She might never have realized that the only thing she had to fear was fear itself.

"I'm too old"

If you're on the other side of fifty, you may be telling yourself you've already missed your chance. "I can't start anything new at my age. Reinvention is a young person's game." But "old" doesn't mean what it used to—not even in a place that celebrates youth the way Hollywood does. Nicole Kidman, now in her early fifties, recently told a reporter that, for actresses, "there isn't a shelf life like there used to be. That's why it's so important to keep changing. We live longer now, if we're fortunate. So there has to be a place to put all that creative energy." Exactly.

Many older people are risk-averse, though, and reinvention always involves some degree of risk, whether it's a personal sea change, like getting remarried, or a professional one, like launching a new business. Some people think, *Oh, but I can't take risks at this stage of life—I have too much to lose!* Think about how bleak that sentiment is. It means that you plan to eke out the last ten, twenty, thirty years of your life in a state of preservation rather than growth. That strikes me as insanely risky: you risk becoming a monument to your former self. But surely your former self learned at some point that fear can be overcome, failure is survivable, and there are no rewards without risks. Don't you want to keep experiencing that high that comes from putting yourself out there and trying something new? Why would you ever willingly give up that feeling?

I look at the age equation this way: the older you are, and the unhappier you feel, the more urgent it is to find a new sense of purpose or a new direction. You don't want to waste another minute.

Luckily, the clock doesn't run out on reinvention, and in some key respects it actually gets easier as time goes on. For one thing, you have more experience coping with change. I remember when I couldn't imagine using anything but a rotary dial phone to communicate over a long distance. Now I text, which has transformed the way I express myself, as well as the amount and type of contact I have with friends and family. I'm an old hand when it comes to adapting to new technologies and cultural trends, and if you can remember life before e-mail, so are you. You've probably also reinvented yourself a time or two, even if you never called it that. Knowing that you've been there, done that, should boost your confidence, not deflate it. You already know the drill, even if you haven't figured out your next incarnation yet.

Remember, you don't have to wipe the slate clean and start all over again from square one. Reinvention is all about who you already are and what you already know. It means calling on your talents, wisdom and experience, and putting them to different uses. Being older, then, can be a real strength: experience is something you probably have in spades, and it's highly valuable—you just have to figure out to whom. That said, ageism is a very real phenomenon, and men over fifty tend to be viewed even more warily than women of the same age, usually because of concerns that they won't be willing to pay their dues or take direction, or will have unrealistic salary expectations. Eagerness and humility are therefore very important. If you're trying to break into a new field or applying for a different kind of job than you've ever held before, it's never a bad idea to acknowledge that you're probably overqualified in some areas but have a lot to learn in others. The key is to frame your experience as an asset while letting it be known that you're not stuck in the past. You're a person who's humble enough to change gears and excited to learn about this new world.

Reinvention isn't always about paid work, though. Maybe you want to study something that's always interested you, or volunteer for a cause that's close to your heart, or pursue a dream that you put on the back burner earlier in life, in which case, take inspiration from the legions of baby boomers who have already pulled off those kinds of reinventions. Every year, an American organization called Encore.org gives out the Purpose Prize, celebrating the achievements of social entrepreneurs and innovators over the age of sixty. People like Pam Koner, a fashion stylist and producer who created Family-to-Family, a not-for-profit that matches families in need with those who have more than enough; sponsors buy food for economically struggling families and work on literacy with the kids. And Vicki Thomas, a high-powered PR and marketing executive who decided to use her years of fundraising experience to benefit Purple Heart Homes, a charity that provides accessible housing to wounded veterans, first as a volunteer and eventually as chief communications officer. The trick to reinvention is to do what she did: take your strengths and experience and repurpose them.

A few years ago, I was visiting Qualicum Beach, British Columbia, when I passed a small art studio. On impulse, I walked inside and saw stumps and tree branches on the floor and a work table lined with several shiny sculptures, almost like medieval helmets, with jagged edges and gold-painted patterns. They were strange and quite beautiful. The wood turner who had created them, Jason Marlow, picked up one of the half-finished sculptures and flipped it upside down to show me that the object was, in fact, mostly a hunk of raw, untouched wood. From one angle, it looked like a bowl, which is probably what most people would have made out of it. But he'd looked at the piece of wood differently, and recognized in its contours the potential for a stunningly original work of art.

There's no age limit on your ability to do something similar. Think about reinvention as a kaleidoscope: all the pieces are inside you already—it just takes a slight turn, a shift in perspective, for the pieces of your life to form a new pattern.

I've undertaken two major reinventions, at two very different stages of life: one when I was thirty and joined Venture, and one with the overhaul of the company, which started when I was fifty-seven. The main difference was that the first time out I had boundless energy, and the second time I . . . didn't. What I did have, though, was a far deeper understanding of my own industry and the business world in general, as well as much more practice navigating around obstacles. I also knew myself much better. I had a clearer picture of my capabilities, which were definitely greater than they had been thirty years before, as well as my weaknesses, which were—are—still my weaknesses. At the end of the day, this quantum leap in self-awareness made it easier to reinvent when I was closing in on sixty than it had been when I was thirty. I didn't *need* as much energy, because I was better prepared in every way.

"I'm too young"

A startling number of people under thirty—the age at which the world is supposedly yours for the taking—feel stuck and unsure of what to do next. To me, anyway, they say things like, "Tell me what to do with my life. My dad wants me to be a lawyer!" I always ask, "Well, what do *you* want to do? You need to do whatever that is, because at some point, what your dad wants you to do won't matter." Not infrequently, the answer is, "I really don't know. I've been so busy ticking other people's boxes that I've never figured out what I want."

These conversations make me grateful that I grew up when I did, because there was so much less pressure on kids, not least because parents weren't in the habit of obsessively scheduling enrichment opportunities for them. Think about the mixed messages millennials have received. On the one hand, they were told that everyone wins (a ribbon just for showing up at the game!) and that there's no such thing as failure (A is for effort!). Yet they were also told that perfection was their only hope of a good life. By the age of seventeen, they were expected to be on the honour roll, volunteering at an environmental charity after school and, on weekends, solving peace in the Middle East—or else they'd jeopardize their chance of getting into a "good" university. No wonder severe anxiety is now commonplace among teens. What we should be telling all kids is, "Fly. Take risks. Make mistakes. Try new things."

That's what I did, and it made all the difference. I didn't know what I wanted to do work-wise until I was thirty years old. I'd held a couple of dead-end clerical and retail jobs and I'd pursued a few doomed entrepreneurial ventures, like the gift basket business my sister-in-law and I started. We thought it was absolutely revolutionary to put artisanal food products in our gift baskets, and create different baskets for different occasions. We were so convinced our idea was a winner that we invested thousands of dollars in a special machine to imprint our logo on the ribbons we used to tie up our baskets. I laugh when I think about it now, because it was so clearly a bad idea, but I learned a ton from mistakes like that one. I probably learned more from the risks I took and the blunders I made than anything else I did in that period of my life, when I really had no clue what or who I wanted to be when I grew up.

So if you're a millennial who feels uncertain about your future and fearful that taking risks could mess up your life forever, don't despair. Reinvention requires getting comfortable with the notion that you don't always know exactly what's going to work or what's going to happen next. One great thing about your stage of life: false starts are very rarely outright disasters, and you almost always learn something about yourself and the world that's worth knowing.

After a lifetime of "you should do X," it can be hard to think in terms of "I want" or "I wish" or "I must." It takes guts to go off script and figure out how to live for yourself. But there's no reason on earth not to try. You have your unique gifts, your energy, your ability to interpret the world in a fresh way, and lots of time to get it right—all valuable assets. So gather information. Sound out people you admire. Read memoirs—and take note of all the mistakes people admit they made, not just their triumphs. But avoid the "replication" trap. You can't be Drake—be what Drake isn't. By all means, try to be a famous recording artist, just not him. That slot is taken. Make your own slot, one that only you can fit inside.

Most importantly, aim high. Later on, there will be plenty of pressure to compromise and settle and downsize your dreams. There's no other time in life when it's easier to go big than when you're young. So do it: go big.

"But what if I fail?"

Well, I'm not going to lie: you might. Tech start-ups, restaurants, retail—all have a 50 percent or higher failure rate, and your reinvention might be a flop too.

Let's say that you're in your late twenties, with a great job in advertising, and you decide to go back to school to study clinical psychology. You've always been good at helping your friends put their problems into perspective, and everyone says you're a great listener. You do your due diligence, interviewing psychologists about their jobs and reading up on career options. Yup, this is definitely what you should be doing with your life. Amazingly enough, you get accepted into a prestigious American program that fast-tracks mature students, so you don't have to repeat all four years of college. You quit your sixty-hour-a-week job and ride off into the sunset, to much fanfare. Your colleagues are inspired (and envious) that you have the guts to follow your passion.

Just a few months into your reinvention, though, you have a sinking feeling. You're doing well in all your classes, but the research you're required to do doesn't interest you in the slightest. It's like the most boring aspects of your old job times ten, and a lot of the studies you're working on strike you as bogus. More worrisome, when your academic supervisor pushes you into volunteering at a suicide prevention hotline, you find that you just don't know how to calm down someone who's really in crisis. No amount of training helps. It's not at all like listening to a friend complain about her boyfriend. These people are desperate, and you live in fear of saying the thing that will push them over the edge, literally. You start having nightmares, extremely realistic ones, about causing a suicide, not preventing one.

You've made an important discovery: you don't actually *like* talking to people with serious mental health issues, which is pretty much the job description of a clinical psychologist. Some are aggressive and threatening, and they scare you; others come from backgrounds with so much trauma and abuse that you find yourself crying silently while you listen to their stories. Your problem isn't an empathy deficit, but a surplus—you feel their pain so deeply that you can't stay calm and objective enough to help them. You start feeling so awful that you begin seeing a therapist yourself, and she immediately prescribes antidepressants. Oh, and one more thing: you miss making and having money.

As may already be obvious, this is not a hypothetical example. One of my friend's kids went through all this about two years ago. As the first year of her program came to a close, she was miserable but felt trapped. She'd been so lucky to get into the program in the first place, and she'd invested so much in her reinvention, both financially and in terms of her reputation. How could she leave now? The thought of telling her supervisor how she felt made her sick, literally. He would think she was a washout, intellectually. And the thought of slinking back to her hometown with her tail between her legs was mortifying. People would see her as a flake, a dilettante, a quitter. And besides, how could she explain the gap on her CV to a prospective new employer? Fortunately, her father, my friend, listened to this litany of excuses for staying and gently told her that she would be doing a disservice to herself, and to the program. Worrying about what others would think wasn't a good reason to continue on a path that she knew was the wrong one for her. And no one who really knew her and cared about her would ever want her to do that.

There's no shame in trying something, deciding it's not for you and cutting your losses. Frankly, there's also no shame in trying something, giving it your very best shot and failing. The key is to take the lesson and move on with a minimum of self-flagellation.

It's almost never the case that a "failed" reinvention is a complete failure, anyway. Each time you change direction, you increase your value, whether you succeed or not. My friend's daughter, for instance, had no difficulty getting another job—a better one, in fact, because she was much clearer on what she was good at, what she enjoyed doing and where she could add value. In job interviews, instead of dancing around that "lost" year, she was upfront about how it had changed her: living somewhere different and doing something different had broadened her horizons, and spending so much time around undergraduates had given her insight into the mindset of one of the most important target audiences for advertisers. It's worth mentioning that today, two years after that "lost" year, she has doubled her salary and is the point person on her agency's largest account.

So that year wasn't really "lost" at all. If she hadn't had the courage to try to reinvent herself, and then to admit that it wasn't working out, she might always have felt, wrongly, that she was meant to be a psychologist. And as she would be the first to tell you, the attempt strengthened her, as did the "failure." It made her wiser, more mature, more understanding of the difficulties so many people have—and even hungrier for success.

This isn't to say that failing at something feels good. It doesn't. Maybe you've read one of those books about "failing up" or "failing forward," or seen one of those TED talks given by some tech guru who embraced his mistakes, learned from them and went on to make gazillions. But I don't see any point in sugar-coating it: while you're failing, it's the worst feeling in the world. My generation was programmed to dread those angry red scribbles on a school essay and the disappointment on our parents' faces when we messed up, so when you actually did fail at something, it felt apocalyptic. Millennials seem to have a different relationship with failure; that is, they've rarely been permitted to experience it. Failure really packs a wallop when you've been programmed to strive for perfection and have never seen an F before. In other words, no matter how old you are, failing feels bad.

But it's never the end of the story, unless you let it be. Whether your reinvention flares or fizzles, it will renew your passion, your drive and your belief in yourself. Reinvention is kind of like compound interest, only for people, not money. You will know more about the world and about your own capabilities. You will know that change is not as terrifying as you might have imagined, failure is not catastrophic, and you are braver than you thought. And because you will be more in touch with your own untapped talents and unrealized ambitions, when the next opportunity rolls around, you'll be ready and willing to reinvent yourself all over again.

"But what if I succeed?"

You may worry that any attempt to reinvent yourself will provoke criticism and resentment, and alienate your friends. Unfortunately, this fear is not unfounded, as anyone who's spent five minutes on social media already knows. Striving to do something different, and do it well, seems to unleash the haters, especially if they can hate on you anonymously. It's happened to me. It's happened to everyone in public life. I dare say that if Mother Teresa were still alive, she'd have her own cadre of Twitter trolls.

I used to think that the more successful you were in life, the more insulated you'd be from criticism and attacks, but I now believe the opposite is true. The tall poppy syndrome, whereby people take glee in trying to cut down anyone who's risen "too far," is a very real phenomenon in Canada. Sometimes the people with the sharpest knives are the ones you thought were your friends, and there's no getting around it: their attacks hurt. A lot.

The silver lining is that there's nothing like success to reveal who's always been in your corner and genuinely wants the best for you. They'll root for you when you try to change, cheer you up when the lows are low, and cheer louder than anyone when the highs are high. So long as you don't become a raging egomaniac, no true friend will begrudge you success.

In any event, the fact that your reinvention may rub some people the wrong way isn't a good reason not to proceed. No one who's accomplished anything difficult or worthwhile has a 100 percent, or even 80 percent, approval rating. Look at it this way: if someone feels threatened by your success, you're probably doing something right.

"I'm not _____ enough"

Whether the concern is not being smart enough, talented enough, connected enough or whatever enough, the core issue is the same: feeling that you don't measure up. Insecurity is not a new phenomenon, of course, but it seems to be so much more toxic in the "selfie" era, when we're inundated with Photoshopped images of other people's beauty and success. It's never been easier to feel "less than."

Whether your dream is to open a restaurant, make a movie, start your own tech company, save the planet or move to Bali, a Google search will reveal people who are already doing it and seem to be miles ahead of you in every way. *What's the point of even trying? Clearly, I don't have the right stuff.*

Sometimes the images are so dazzling that it's hard to remember a key fact: you don't really know a thing about these people. You have no way of knowing what their un-Photoshopped, unfiltered lives are actually like. You have no idea how they feel inside. I'm willing to bet, though, that they don't see themselves as superior beings (and if they do, they're not people you should envy or be intimidated by). Think how many famous and celebrated people have gone public with their mental health struggles, addictions and heartbreaks. It's always a shock, but it shouldn't be: they're only human. They have insecurities too (possibly even more than you have, judging from my own experience with celebrities). Which proves the point: insecurity is no barrier to achievement. It didn't stand in their way and it shouldn't stand in yours either.

A touch of self-doubt can actually fuel a reinvention, in much the same way that a touch of anxiety or stage fright has been shown to improve performance, because it makes you that much more alert. Self-doubters tend to work harder, because they've got something to prove but don't have full confidence in their ability to prove it. If anything, they tend to be overachievers. How do I know all this? I have my own insecurities, of course. But I've come to view them as performance enhancers, spurs to try harder, rather than excuses not to try at all.

Frankly, if you really think you're not good enough in some way, the last thing you should be doing is nothing. You should be going all out to try to get better at whatever it is that makes you insecure, so that you get strong enough to take the next step.

You're not excused

The prospect of change can be frightening, especially if you didn't really want to change but circumstances have left you no choice—your job is gone, or your relationship is finished, or there's been a flood, and life as you knew it is now over. But change is also an opportunity: to chase a dream, to build a better life for yourself, to be happier and more fulfilled than you are today.

You have a chance to write a whole new kind of story for yourself. Depending on your starting point, that could mean the difference between a full, colourful life and one that feels empty and grey. If you don't try, you'll never know how far you could have gone, or what heights you could have scaled. And you might never get over the disappointment and sense of loss. I'm sure you know at least one guy who's still crying in his beer about the shot he didn't take, way back when, and how different his life could have been. How he could have been a contender.

You don't want to be that guy. And you don't have to be. You can choose a new kind of future, one where you bet on yourself—and live for yourself. But it *is* up to you. You are the only person who can change your own life.

Chapter 2

The time is now

If those four words scare the living daylights out of you, I get it. I'm not so comfortable turning on a dime and taking risks either—unless the potential of a reward feels very real. If you've ever watched *Dragons' Den*, you may be under the impression that I'm a daredevil who gambles wildly on young companies and novel ideas. Well, that's the magic of editing for television, where all the boring bits wind up on the cutting room floor. While it's true that I've invested more money and closed more deals than any of the other Dragons in the history of the show, it's also true that a surprising number have fallen apart after the cameras stopped rolling. During due diligence, I sometimes discover that an entrepreneur inflated his sales or fudged her numbers, in which case I'm out. In fact, if anything I discover doesn't match up to the bill of goods I was sold when the cameras were rolling, I'm out. I've worked way too hard for my money to be careless with it.

Similarly, I am cautious in my personal life. With age has come a little wisdom, at least about myself. I've learned the hard way that I have a tendency to trust others before they've earned it, and I know now to hold myself back until I'm really sure about another person.

All of which is to say that I'd be the last person to advise you to throw caution to the winds and start taking crazy risks. Frankly, some risks—catastrophic financial loss, endangering your own health, jeopardizing your relationship with your children, compromising your own values and beliefs—are never worth taking, no matter how big the potential reward.

But when you're contemplating changing your life in some significant way, the risk that should be top of mind is the risk of regret. Ask yourself: if I don't try to chart a new course, will I spend the rest of my life regretting it? Regret, and the self-pity and bitter disappointment that so often go along with it, is like a slow-acting poison. It shrivels you up inside in a way that loss, embarrassment or outright failure never could.

Regret is also a complete waste of time, so I try not to obsess over my own less than stellar decisions. Sure, if time travel were possible, there are plenty of things in my life that I would go back and do differently. But beating yourself up about choices and events you can't change accomplishes nothing—except stopping you from looking forward at all the ways you can try to do better.

Preventing regret, however, is another story. That's a forward-looking activity, and an excellent investment of time. Not that it takes very long; most of us, even in the throes of agonizing over a decision, are crystal clear on which path we'd regret not having taken, a year or two down the road. Usually, it's the steeper, more daunting one, the one that will demand much more of you and therefore induces more self-doubt.

My own biggest business mistakes have always involved turning away from those really daunting climbs and reining in my own ambition. I listened to that voice inside saying, *Who do you think you are?* I'll never know what I might have been capable of if I had managed to silence it when I was younger, and pushed myself to strive to achieve more. If I ever say that out loud, though, the response is usually something like, "But look at everything you've done!" To which my reply is, "Just think what else I *could* have done." I don't feel regret, exactly, but rather an awareness of missed opportunities, either because I didn't dream big enough or because I didn't have the courage of my convictions.

You may have to do some homework

Case in point: When I bought out my partners and became CEO of Venture, in the late nineties, I wanted to expand the company, but we were limited by our location. The major national and multinational accounts always seemed to land in Toronto or Montreal, even though there were a lot of excellent regional marketing agencies operating in the West. We were all in our silos, however, squabbling over the same scraps of business.

I had an idea: what if we consolidated to form a kind of western Canadian super-agency, one that could compete with Toronto and Montreal? That's what had happened in the United States, where big shops had been busy acquiring smaller, highly creative firms and winning all the industry awards. There was no reason we couldn't do the same thing. Sure, it would necessitate a reinvention of the way we did business. But if it worked, it would be so worth it.

Well, it didn't happen. I quasi-tried to raise the capital we'd need for such an ambitious undertaking, but gave up quickly. Shame on me, because I went out looking for money in a haphazard way, but in my own defence, I also faced a fair amount of sexism. This was the nineties, and there's no question that women in business were viewed differently then. I remember pitching to a roomful of men and seeing only amusement on their faces, like "Oh, how cute!" The condescension was subtle, but real.

An even more powerful factor working against me, though, was my lack of faith in myself. On some level, I wasn't fully convinced of the value of my idea, primarily because it *was* my idea. My internal critic, the same one that talked a blue streak every time I gained a pound or two, kept telling me that I didn't know what I was talking about. *So now you think you're some kind of marketing genius who can see what no one else can see?* I should have ignored that voice, but I didn't. I tuned in to it and then cranked up the volume, to the point where every "no" from a prospective funder made perfect sense. Instead of strengthening my resolve to succeed, rejection strengthened my belief that that critical little voice I could hear in my head was dispensing pearls of wisdom. My reinvention plan *was* stupid.

So let's sum up: I saw the market opportunity. I set up a handful of meetings. But after a few no's, I gave up on reinvention. I defeated myself before anyone else had a chance to do it.

That wasn't the end of the story, though. Five years later, a couple of men consolidated Canadian marketing in exactly the way I'd proposed. They had a strong pitch, and they secured the capital. And, by the way, the concept was a winner. They did very, very well.

You may be thinking that the moral of this story is that I was ahead of my time. But there was nothing wrong with my timing; I'm certain consolidation would have been successful if I'd managed to sell anyone else on it. The problem was my approach. I needed to provide more evidence that this was a really good idea. The fact that consolidation had worked somewhere else wasn't enough to sell it here (just look at Target, a massive American retail success that failed miserably on this side of the border). I needed to be able to articulate why it would fly in our market, and how we could tweak the model to take regional peculiarities into account.

At the first or second "no," if I hadn't been listening to my inner critic, I might have realized that I needed to do a bit more homework: speak to American marketers about their experiences; run the numbers on cost savings to smaller firms; deconstruct a pitch lost to the big boys in Toronto, say, to show how, together, we Westerners could have won it. If I had done that, it would have strengthened my confidence in myself and my idea, and given me the ammunition I needed to pitch it more effectively and defend it more tenaciously.

But to me, the opportunity felt so urgent that my top priority was to get others to buy in to the concept. A lack of confidence may have been at play here too. In retrospect, I think I probably wanted other people to validate my idea because, as a new CEO, I was still learning to believe in my own vision. In any event, I thought there'd be plenty of time later on to fill in all the details and finer points. Or, to put it another way, I put the cart before the horse. No wonder no one else wanted to jump on board.

This is a mistake I sometimes see others make when they're pitching me. They're excited by their brainstorm for a product or a start-up or a whatever, and they begin trying to line up support for it too soon. They think that simply painting the picture in very broad strokes will be enough to get me excited too. But a sketch, even of the Taj Mahal, is still just a sketch. Investors want some idea of how you're going to build the thing, what materials you plan to use, how many workers you think you'll need, and so on. You don't need to be able to describe the shrubbery lining the path you're asking investors to walk with you, but you do need a good sense of its general direction. You have to be able to articulate your vision, even if you haven't fully worked it out yet, because no one else can see what you see.

Depending on the nature of your reinvention, then, you may need to put in some work before taking action. Note the word "some": there's a thick and unmistakable line between good-enough preparation and over-preparation. Research is always a good idea, but you don't need to memorize the encyclopedia. In my case, a week or two of research would've been plenty. I just needed more ammunition for those initial meetings with investors, not a whole war plan. If that week or two had dragged into months, I wouldn't have been preparing, I would've been procrastinating.

So if you have a big dream, and you're standing at the bottom of the mountain looking up at a steep, daunting path, by all means take a little time to be sure you've got the supplies you need and figure out the best angle of attack. But don't dither too long. You may think you're "getting ready" or "ensuring success through preparation," but you're not. Instead of leaping a tad too early, as I did, you're procrastinating, and that is something you will regret.

Procrastination is more painful than change

I once posed an open question on Twitter: "What is your biggest regret?" The answers blew in like a hurricane (regret seems to have the same kind of destructive power, too). "Biggest regret: living with the idea day in and out that I am destined for more, but just can't materialize or visualize what that is . . . at 37." "I scolded my dad over something really stupid. He died a couple hours later. I never got to reconcile." "Not taking off more time when my children were born." The regrets were all specific, but they were also all the same: *I wish I had been all that I know in my heart I could have been.*

What really astonished me, though, was how many people's regrets touched not on their failure to achieve a goal—they'd achieved it, all right—but on how long they'd put off taking the first steps. They'd known what they wanted to do but hadn't taken action. "My biggest regret: not following my passion from the very beginning. Letting others dictate my direction in life." "Not starting our own business sooner." "Laziness and procrastination. Getting too comfortable and not pushing myself." "Every time I've ever doubted myself. I wish I had been confident and had faith in myself that I would accomplish my goal."

Not one person said, "You know, I really wish I'd dawdled a little longer before going after my dream." What people regret is dawdling, period, once they'd made up their minds to change their lives for the better.

So why wait? Nine times out of ten, the explanation is some version of "I just don't feel ready." If you're the kind of person who over-rehearses and over-prepares for every meeting or presentation, to the point where an unexpected question throws you off track, "getting ready" can be a laborious and time-consuming affair that fills however many days, weeks and months you allot to it.

For some people, procrastination is an art form. We all know someone who's been floating a trial balloon forever. He has an idea—and it might even be a really good idea—but it never moves beyond the conceptual stage, and never will. That doesn't bother him, though. He enjoys noodling around on the Internet, "researching." For him, it's like fantasy football: an enjoyable diversion.

For everyone else, procrastination is self-inflicted torture. Whatever you're putting off never really vanishes from your mind. It's always there, nagging at you, making you feel bad about yourself. It's particularly painful when what you're procrastinating about is changing your life for the better. Now, on top of your dissatisfaction with your life, you also have to deal with the guilt and shame of knowing that you're not doing anything about it.

Procrastination is such a big problem for so many people that researchers all over the world study the phenomenon, and what they've discovered is that procrastination feels worse—significantly worse, usually—than doing whatever it is you've been procrastinating about. In other words, whatever you're feeling right now is more painful than change will be. You've built change up to be the most difficult, painful thing in the world, but it's not. Procrastinating about change is the most difficult, painful thing.

Another finding: it's easier to stop procrastinating when a task is broken down into smaller chunks. For instance, instead of telling yourself for the eighteenth time that you're going to do your taxes today, and this time you really mean it, try this: "First I'll dig up last year's return, then find all my receipts for deductions, then locate my RRSP contribution slip" and so on. Experiencing the gratification of completion as you knock off each small chunk helps you keep going. This is one reason the plan we use to help companies reinvent themselves works. We don't charge in yelling, "Let's shake everything up, pronto!" Rather, there's a methodical process, with discrete steps and stages. And with every step, momentum increases, along with confidence, which makes it easier to carry on.

For the same reasons, having a plan is going to help you. The hardest step is undoubtedly the first one: just getting going. But once you do, the pain of procrastination will be behind you, and you'll also be on your way to preventing the pain of regret.

Perfectionism is a form of procrastination

Here's the thing: no one ever feels completely ready for change. And people who are comfortable with change say it's actually better *not* to feel ready.

Waiting for perfect conditions is a mug's game, according to my friend Annette Verschuren, and she should know. She's the powerhouse who took Home Depot Canada from nineteen stores to 179, then introduced the chain to China, and is now the CEO of an innovative energy storage company. An expert when it comes to reinvention, she worked in coal mining before bringing Michaels, the craft store, to Canada, with a stint along the way in financial services and, oh yeah, a gig privatizing Crown corporations. She describes herself as "a builder, not a maintainer," so when she feels she's built something up as far as she can, she's out of there and off to her next incarnation. Her motto: "mediocre strategy, great execution." She never waits to feel 100 percent ready—she starts executing, she says, when 60 to 70 percent of the pieces of the puzzle are in place. Waiting for that perfect 100 percent would mean getting started too late.

If you want to be the best in the world at something, perfectionism can be an asset. Serena Williams, for instance, attributes her success to perfectionism, and it's hard to argue with a track record like hers. But even for superstars, perfectionism can also be a curse. Prima ballerina Karen Kain, for instance, has written about experiencing depression in her twenties, when the perfectionism that helped vault her to stardom started backfiring. "I became preoccupied with performing well," she explained, "which only led to doubting my own abilities and a further loss of confidence."

That's what perfectionism does to most people: it creates anxiety and self-doubt, which can shut you down before you even get started. One of my very first jobs was as a secretary at Alberta Government Telephones, where I worked for a woman named Irene. She was the assistant to what we then called a "fifth level"—now we'd say CEO—and I was assistant to her. Irene wore perfectly pressed skirts and did not suffer fools or errors. I was terrified of her. She had a bloodhound's nose for typos, and if a tab was indented one extra space, she'd hand whatever I'd typed right back for a do-over. (This was in the pre-computer era, when a do-over meant retyping the entire page, which meant you might make a whole new set of mistakes.) Like a disappointed schoolteacher, she'd sometimes return a letter I'd typed with the mistakes circled in red ink. So I was very excited when Wite-Out was brought into the office—but Irene would not let us use it. She thought we ought to strive for perfection, and achieve it without the help of a "crutch." Well, I became so scared of making mistakes that I started making even more of them, and got less and less done every day. As you may already have guessed, my career at the phone company was short-lived.

I think of Irene when I find myself obsessing over minutiae and getting in my own way. Being reasonably well-prepared (the way I should have been when pitching consolidation), and ready to make corrections when necessary, is good enough when what you're trying to do is get something started or change direction. "Women especially always want to be perfect, and it's bullshit," as Annette Verschuren puts it. "We lose ideas that way. Wait until it's perfect and guess what? The guys get the jump on us. Women need to be more comfortable taking greater risks faster."

Men do seem to find it easier to get going on a big change even when they don't feel entirely ready. There are plenty of male perfectionists out there, to be sure, but men are socialized differently: they're encouraged to take bold risks, and to view a little sloppiness as not only acceptable but manly. Asim Qureshi, co-founder of a start-up I invested in, is a case in point. Figuring there was no way to plan for every contingency, he jumped in at the deep end, quitting his high-flying corporate job before his halal food company was even close to being a sure thing.

"The biggest lesson I've learned is that if the goal is a thousand steps away, you don't actually take a thousand steps," he says. "You make a plan, then you take the first, the second and the third steps, and all of a sudden five and six will reveal themselves. Then you do eight, nine, ten, eleven, twelve, and the guy you met at thirteen knows someone who will help you at step sixteen." In other words, connections and insights arise along the way and accelerate the process—yet another reason to get going sooner rather than later. "There's an idea in Islam that if you take a step

toward God, He will take ten steps toward you," Qureshi continues. "I feel it's been the same with starting the company. Things
happen that aren't intentional, and that's what's so beautiful about
the journey."

Perfectionism takes the focus away from the journey and feeds
the fantasy that you can control all outcomes. I've learned over
and over that that's simply not possible. There's no way to anticipate everything that will happen, so there's no point waiting
until you feel perfectly ready. I know people who swear by Excel
spreadsheets and business models, but I don't put a ton of faith
in theoretical models because I've seen, far too many times, how
often everything swerves off course in real life. A model works
only if people behave exactly as they say they will, and human
behaviour is never that predictable.

For meticulous planners and perfectionists, ambiguity can be
unsettling. But if you wait until conditions are absolutely perfect
and you feel 100 percent ready, you may be waiting a very, very
long time. And that is something you will almost certainly come
to regret.

Go ahead, expose yourself

So far, I've been talking about reinventions with happy origins.
Many do start that way, sparked by the scent of a great business
opportunity, or a desire to switch careers, or an opportunity to pull
up stakes and move, or the arrival of a baby, or finally having the
time and/or money to pursue a dream that's been simmering on
the back burner for years. In other cases, reinvention is triggered
by some version of disaster, as mine was: an economic downturn,

a layoff, a serious illness, a breakup. And in that case, the reasons for procrastination may be a little different. You might be tempted to delay because, in order to take the first step toward a new kind of life, you have to be willing to let the world discover that you're unhappy, or that you feel unfulfilled, or that you've given plan A your best shot but it just hasn't worked out.

Admitting any of that can feel unbearably embarrassing, especially if it runs counter to the version of events that you've been posting on Instagram. Inquiring minds will want to know why you're suddenly changing your story. "You broke off your engagement? I thought you said he was a great guy, and you couldn't wait to get married." "Wait a sec—you're quitting?! But didn't you say you were in line for a big promotion?" And so forth. It's important to remember that often these questions are innocent. If you're embarking on a 180-degree turn, it's understandable that people may be a little confused.

However, it's also true that there's sometimes a needling quality to the curiosity, and something almost gleeful in the expressions of "concern." You may also hear a few variations on the theme of "I told you so." Being judged is not pleasant, even at the best of times, but it's especially unpleasant when you already feel tentative and vulnerable. The mere prospect of judgment could be enough to make you decide to postpone making changes to your life. You might entertain fantasies that if you just wait a while, you'll be able to short-circuit negative judgment altogether. "Being passed over for that promotion was the best thing that ever happened to me, because guess what? I landed a new job, and it's in Paris!"

I understand the temptation to postpone feeling judged, because in those first horrible months after the flood, I really, really didn't want anyone to find out that my company was in serious trouble. It's still very difficult and almost physically painful for me to admit that, and it will be news to my team; to this day, they don't know just how bad it was or just how close I came to shutting the business down altogether. At the time, they knew that I was risking my own capital to keep the company afloat, but they probably underestimated what it was costing me, and money was the least of it.

The shame of having let people down, and of having failed the company I owed my career to, was almost insurmountable. A few people had to know just how severe the crisis was—my banker, who repeatedly urged me to cut my losses and close the business; Venture's chief financial officer, who was overwhelmed by the stress of balancing payables when we had so little money coming in—but I didn't want the team to find out. I was already staggering through the days under the weight of my guilt. At night, when I thought of how disappointed in me they'd be if they knew the true state of affairs, and how much less respect they'd have for me as a leader, I'd have terrible panic attacks, gulping for breath. My heart would be beating so fast that I'd feel as if I was going to die, and mentally I'd negotiate: "Hey God, not now, okay?"

I worried, too, that if the team knew the whole truth, even more of them would leave, and then we'd lose those clients who had loyally stuck with us, and the whole house of cards would come tumbling down. So I couldn't show anyone how afraid I was. The team was counting on me, our clients were counting on me, and the bank was counting on me to repay the loans I'd taken to make payroll.

It was one of the loneliest times of my life, and through it all I was trying to hold my head up and pretend that nothing was wrong. The cognitive dissonance was extreme. There I was on *Dragons' Den*, instructing entrepreneurs on the finer points of running a company, all the while terrified that I was about to lose mine and, along with it, my identity as a person who could overcome obstacles. What was my value in the world if I wasn't strong and successful? I could imagine the snide asides all too easily: *What kind of Dragon can't even keep her own company afloat?*

However, Venture really was in a life-or-death situation. I knew that if I dragged my feet on making changes because I was squeamish about feeling exposed, the company would fail altogether. So I got going on trying to save it. I didn't broadcast our troubles, and I definitely downplayed them, but you didn't have to be a sleuth to figure out that we'd downsized—and when companies downsize, it's never good news. But surprise: feeling vulnerable wasn't as awful as I'd thought it would be, partly because I was way too busy reinventing the company to focus on the discomfort. Furthermore, people who had a sense of what was going on were generally supportive.

This shouldn't have surprised me, really, because when someone reveals vulnerability to me, my instinct is to be encouraging and provide support. In fact, I usually feel more closely connected to that person—especially if, prior to that moment, I'd thought of him or her as tough, resilient and successful. Think about it: moments when strong, powerful people reveal their vulnerability can be deeply moving. A few years ago, Adele performed after a year's hiatus. I watched her on TV as she nailed her set with the biggest voice in the world. Then she stood there with tears in her eyes, admitting to millions of viewers that she'd been terrified. She'd been worried that no one cared about her anymore. Her confession only brought the audience closer. *Oh*, we thought, *she's human after all.*

When you're in the thick of it, about to embark on real change, you can get a little paranoid, and forget that *everyone* feels fragile at times. You're not experiencing some bizarre, embarrassing affliction that will make people run down the street howling with laughter if they find out. Admitting that you're not happy or you're full of self-doubt won't be read as a sign of weakness; it will be seen as a sign that you're human. And deciding to course-correct isn't a declaration of defeat; it's a declaration of courage.

Don't let embarrassment or fear of judgment tempt you to delay changing your life for the better. When you've experienced some kind of setback and really do need to change, deferring it only makes matters worse. Besides, you don't really lose when other people judge you. You gain, in a way, because your judges have exposed their true colours: they don't wish you well. That's valuable information, and you should act on it as part of your reinvention.

Toxic shock

A frenemy—a saboteur disguised as an ally—could be a friend, a relative, a boss or (sorry to say) a husband, wife, partner. Bottom line: this is someone who already drains your courage and undermines your confidence, and therefore has the power to scare you right out of trying to chart a new course for yourself.

This is another one of those hard lessons I learned first-hand. For a few years, I was close to one of those bright-light people whom everyone is drawn to. We hit it off. I had an inkling that the way my friend behaved in her professional life wasn't the same way that I behaved, but I was so captivated by her liveliness and intelligence that I did a bit of a don't-ask-don't-tell, and didn't investigate too deeply. I'm not proud of that fact.

Despite the fun we had, she was a genius at both inducing and exacerbating self-doubt. "Really? *Him?*" she'd say, raising an eyebrow, when I started dating someone new. Her manipulations were subtle, and always disguised as concern: "I just hope he treats you well. I don't get the sense that he's all that into you. I don't want you to get hurt. Again." She'd leave me reeling with uncertainty about my own judgment, and my own worth, and that much more hungry for her "support."

Over time, the red flags became less easy to ignore. I learned that she had used my name to get ahead professionally, without checking with me first. And once, I overheard her telling someone else about my second divorce, describing in detail how, in the aftermath, I'd struggled with depression. It was a difficult episode that I had shared with her in confidence, and I was mortified to hear it being reduced to cocktail party chatter. I also didn't recognize the person she was describing. She painted a picture of me as pathetically weak and damaged. *Is that* me? I wondered. Of course it wasn't, but by that point she was really affecting how I saw myself. It felt as if something toxic, an infectious agent, was leaching directly into my bloodstream.

When I checked in with her after these incidents, though, she laughed them off. "You're so sensitive, Arlene! That's not what I meant at all." I can see now that I was being gaslighted, but I didn't get it then. I'm a better judge of people in my professional life than I am in my personal life, and I was willing to give her the benefit of the doubt. Maybe I *was* too sensitive. Maybe it *wasn't* such a big deal.

When Venture was in real trouble, I was too embarrassed to disclose to her just how bad things were (another red flag, a big one—this woman was supposed to be my friend, for goodness' sake!) or that I was planning to reinvent the company. What little

I told her elicited just enough "concern" to make me start second-guessing myself. Did I really have what it took to right the ship? Was the company really worth saving?

Then I learned that she had once again badmouthed me in a professional setting. That was it, as far as I was concerned. I finally connected the dots and understood that she wasn't the person I'd thought she was. But it's hard to separate from toxic people, especially when you're feeling vulnerable and you're trying to do something as difficult as changing your life. The relationships run deep, because frenemies encourage dependency, then maintain it by making you feel so bad about yourself that you're just grateful to have this wonderful friend who loves you anyway. Often, too, you've invested so much in the relationship that leaving it feels like failure. (Here's a good litmus test of toxicity: the relationship leaves you feeling drained rather than energized, yet, like a gambler, you keep thinking that if you just invest a little more time and energy, you can turn it around.)

This is where your courage has to kick in. You want to change your life? Start now. Pull away from anybody who makes you feel weak or incompetent or in any way reinforces your self-doubt. Those feelings will encourage you to delay reinvention, and will also impair your ability to proceed if you manage to get started. Whether the issue is that your frenemy is envious, or controlling, or deeply insecure, or just a garden-variety mean girl (or boy), all grown up, doesn't matter. What does matter is that toxic people are experts at picking up on and affirming the negative things you already believe about yourself. Oh, they know how to push our buttons! And they will push them like crazy after you confide that you're about to try to change direction. Frenemies don't want you to do that; they know that change threatens the dynamic of the relationship—they may wind up with less power over you.

Make sure that happens. If you've decided to improve your life, you need people around you who will support, not thwart, you. Who makes you feel the most like yourself? Who brings out the best in you? Those are the people you need in your corner, the true friends who buoy your confidence and celebrate your victories.

Now, take some names in the true sense of "taking names": Is there someone who makes you feel small or stupid? Who fills you with self-doubt? Who is occupying a friend slot in your life but doesn't leave you feeling the way a friend should (see paragraph above)?

If this were the movies, you'd confront your frenemy (I hope there's only one), hash out your differences Kumbaya-style and reinvent your friendship. But in reality, hashing things out only makes sense if you want to hang on to the friendship. I wanted my frenemy out of my life; the sad truth was that she'd never really been much of a friend to me, and I feared her ability to destabilize me when I needed to keep plowing ahead with Venture's reinvention. So I opted for self-preservation rather than bravery, went quiet after explaining that I was very busy (it was the truth), and things eventually petered out. I knew that a big blowout would only be painful, not cathartic, and I was already in plenty of pain. I was so hurt and felt terribly betrayed by this person who had been a pillar in my life. Friendship breakups are often even more devastating than romantic ones, because you never suspect it could happen.

When you're changing your life, you need to be sure that everyone in your circle has your back and wishes you well. It's amazing how even a small gesture of support can reinforce your intentions and bolster your willpower. A few years ago, in San Diego, I ran a half-marathon. The then-president of Venture did something amazingly thoughtful: she ordered a bracelet for me with a motivational saying on it, and it was waiting for me when I checked into my hotel. I was really touched by this show of support, and by her recognition that this race meant a lot to me (and would be hard for me, too). I was also touched by all the strangers standing at the side of the route. Of course there would be long periods when I was running without a cheering section, my body aching and my spirit flagging. And then, all of a sudden, a single person would appear with a cowbell or a poster (*Wine at the finish line!*), clapping and yelling encouragement. It always gave me a little burst of adrenalin. I was instantly lifted.

So at the same time that you're excising any toxic elements from your life, also figure out who wants you to succeed, and hold them close. They will make you feel more confident and help you run faster.

It's about time

You don't have to be perfect. You don't have to feel 100 percent ready. You don't have to be scared or embarrassed to admit that you're not satisfied with your life and want more. All you have to be is willing to do some homework and ready to figure out who you really are and how to capitalize on that.

One benefit of the reinvention process is that the first few steps involve looking inward and taking inventory, not making sudden, irreversible moves. As you figure out the direction you should take, you're also building confidence, which in turn strengthens resolve. You *will* change your life for the better.

And for that, there's no time like the present.

Part Two

GOING BACKWARDS

To understand how and why the reinvention process you're about to embark on actually works, you first need to know a little bit about marketing. This won't be painful, I promise, and the core concepts are ones you need to understand so you can implement them yourself.

Let's start at the beginning, with the way we create a marketing strategy. When clients come to Venture, they might have a great product and have been churning away, but they're not growing; or, they might be growing all right, but they're experiencing competitive pressure and it's forced them to re-evaluate their prospects. Usually, they've been trying to do their marketing on their own on a shoestring budget, without really understanding how to communicate the value of their products to the right people, or else they've been working with another firm and it hasn't really panned out.

Our role is to help create a brand identity that encapsulates both what the company's purpose is in the world and what unique benefits its products offer. Clear transmission of a company's values and sense of purpose is key to creating a connection with consumers; it's why you feel an emotional pull toward a particular brand in the grocery store and no substitute will do. You trust that company. You're loyal to that brand not just because of the particular features of its products but because of everything the brand stands for.

Think about Volvo for a moment. You don't buy a Volvo because the rubber used for its tires is better than the rubber another car company uses, or because it handles well in the rain, or because the seats are super comfortable, or because it's less expensive than a car with similar features, though all those things might be true. You buy it because you care about safety. The company's core purpose—keeping people safe—aligns with your own values and beliefs. How do you know that? Marketing, to a large extent.

When a brand's identity is really well-established and authentically reflects reality, you can sum up what it stands for in a word or two. With Volvo, what's the first word that comes to mind? "Safety," right? Absolutely everything the company does reinforces that it's all about safety. They tout their investments in new technology to make their vehicles even safer; their ads often feature children, to drive home the point that this is the car you buy if you care about protecting your family. They've branched out successfully, creating new products that are all about safety: child car seats, new types of car lights and so forth.

A brand identity is what a corporation and marketers work together to create. But a *brand* itself exists in the eye of the beholder: it's everything you think and feel when you see a Volvo.

If your friend who drives one is sideswiped by a truck but walks away without a scratch, Volvo's brand becomes stronger in your mind. *It really is a safe car.* But—and this is an entirely fictional example—let's say you saw a report showing that the company was aware of a problem with its cars' braking system but did nothing to correct it. That never happened, but let's just pretend it did. Instead of "safety," you'd think of that report when you saw a Volvo approaching a stop sign. It wouldn't matter what some ad tried to tell you; your perception of the brand would change, fundamentally.

This is what marketers mean when they say that perception is reality. I always tell clients, "A brand is really just your company, seen through the eyes of others." You can try to control what others see, through the way you market your products. But ultimately, the best way to protect your brand is simply to be consistent in everything you do. If every interaction people have with your company conveys the same message, whether they're speaking to a receptionist or going on your website or using your product, your brand will be strong. If, however, your people are wearing uniforms that scream "sexy" and your website is hipsterish yet your product is intended for toddlers, you're going to have a problem.

Coming up with a brand identity, then, is not so simple. You can't just make it up. If you want it to stick, it must be authentic and it must reflect reality. Therefore, when a company hires us, we need to do a deep dive to see for ourselves what the organization is all about. We can't just take the CEO's word for it that this is an awesome organization that makes amazing stuff. We need to know what's true and what's wishful thinking—and if there's a lot of wishful thinking going on, it's our job to point out the ways the company should reinvent from within, before we can start marketing it.

To figure out what's actually going on in an organization, we start by looking at its records, interviewing company insiders and surveying outsiders, to get an accurate, 360-degree picture of the place. That usually takes twelve to sixteen weeks, which can feel like an eternity if the company is in dire straits. Implementing a new brand strategy and communicating it—via advertising, social media and so on—takes much longer. It's not so easy to get people's attention these days, when we're all being bombarded with thousands of messages, images, news snippets and opinions from the second we turn on our phones in the morning. A couple of billboards and some eye-catching magazine ads just won't cut it anymore. Really establishing an identity for a new brand, or transforming an existing brand, requires a multi-pronged approach and a smart strategy.

But how we start is always the same: by going backwards. That's what you have to do to figure out how to go forward.

Chapter 3

Who do you think you were?

Once you've sold yourself on the idea of changing your own life, you're ready to begin figuring out which directions are open to you. If you already have a pretty clear idea where you want to go, great. But as I tell clients who are champing at the bit to get started on a brand reinvention, there are no shortcuts to a better future.

Before a brand can be steered in a new direction, we need to be clear on what it stands for, and how and why it came to be—its history, in other words. Sometimes a client listens to this, not so patiently, then says something like, "Look, I don't have time for navel-gazing. How about you just cut to the chase and tell me how to sell more widgets already?"

It doesn't work that way, in marketing or in life. Remember: Reinvention is not about fabricating a new identity out of whole cloth, or faking it in hopes of making it. It's about building on what you already have and who you already are. And you can't do that unless you actually know who you are, inside and out. Self-awareness is the secret sauce of any reinvention.

So when we're developing a brand identity or repositioning an existing brand, we ask to see old business plans, financial information, previous marketing plans, old logos, ads—if clients can dig it up, we want to see it. Sometimes they protest that this exercise seems like a colossal waste of time. *We need to focus on the future, not the past!*

But companies, just like people, can and do lose their way as time passes. Often, rediscovering and recommitting to first principles is the first step to a resurgence. Even the most successful companies need to understand their history, because a brand's values should remain consistent over time. That's how you earn consumers' trust: they know what you stand for, and they also know they can count on you.

Paradoxically, then, change begins by looking backwards. In order to figure out where you can go, you need to know exactly where you've been. So we ask questions, a lot of them. Why was this company started in the first place—what was the dream? What was it going to offer that no one else could? What were the founders' core values? What were they fighting against—competitors' high prices, or poor quality, or manufacturing practices, or . . . ? Going back to first principles strips away the cynicism and disappointments that have accrued over time, and helps insiders see the company and its products in a new light.

There's another reason to do it too: the seeds of a successful reinvention are often found in the past. I'd seen this time and again when working with other companies, but when I realized we needed to reinvent Venture, I thought I could afford to skip the walk down memory lane. After all, I already knew the company's history inside out. I'd worked there most of my adult life.

Instead, I jumped ahead a couple of steps and took a quick inventory of all our assets. On the left-hand side of a whiteboard I scribbled a list of our existing clients. On the right-hand side there was youinc.com, a digital platform we'd created to help entrepreneurs connect with each other and find the education, resources and tools they need to succeed. Below that, I wrote down all the things I did on my own—TV work, writing books, investing in start-ups and early-stage companies, giving speeches about entrepreneurship—that helped Venture by boosting its visibility. When I stood back to look at the big picture, the disconnect between the left and right sides of the board was striking. The names on the left were traditional and corporate; the activities on the right were all about entrepreneurs who were trying to do things in a new way. It was striking, too, that each project was in its own silo, separate from the rest. How had that happened?

Oh. Apparently, a review of the past would be helpful after all. Just as I tell clients, there are no shortcuts. Unfortunately, I couldn't dig up old annual reports and campaigns we'd done back in the day. A lot of our early work existed only on paper, had been stored in filing cabinets in the basement of our building—and was obliterated by the flood. I had to rely on my own memory to reconstruct the company's first years, a rather frightening prospect given how frequently I forget where I've put my car keys. But once I really focused and started jotting down notes, I was amazed by how vivid my recollections were, and also by how much light they shed on our current predicament.

Back to square one

When I started at Venture in the late eighties, many of Canada's biggest marketing and advertising agencies prided themselves on their sophistication. A lot of them were local franchises of huge multinational firms, and they seemed much less interested in delivering for clients than they were in driving bottom-line profits and winning awards to impress the head honcho in New York. Their attitude toward clients sometimes came off as down-right condescending, like, "We're the fancy experts, you're lucky we're deigning to work with you."

By comparison, Venture was, back then, a small-time outfit with strictly local accounts: a car dealership, a dog grooming salon. The slick firms in Toronto would no doubt have viewed our clients, and us, as hicks. But we took our clients very seriously, because we knew they were knocking themselves out to build their companies and support their families, just like we were. We also knew that if we messed up a print ad or a billboard, it could cause real harm—not to some faceless conglomerate with gazillions to spend on marketing, but to a small business owner we were likely to bump into in the supermarket. We rooted for the underdog. We were underdogs too.

We were trying to build a different kind of agency, one that was scrappy and distinctively Western, smart but unpretentious, and 100 percent client-centred. Our goal wasn't to make a killing and win plaques for ourselves, but to do whatever it took to make our clients' companies successful. We wanted to be both highly creative and highly accountable to our clients' business metrics as well as our own; we didn't believe those things were mutually exclusive. Another point of difference: we wanted Venture to be a fun place to work, not a clone of the hierarchical, dog-eat-dog agencies. We worked as hard as they did—harder, probably, because our clients had so much less to spend and we had so many fewer of them—but the vibe in our office was comparatively relaxed, and the camaraderie was unbeatable. You didn't have to worry about anyone stabbing you in the back. We were all in it together.

The challenge of getting a young company up and running made me feel alive and in control of my own life in a way I never had before. I was constantly learning and experimenting and stretching myself. But it wasn't all rainbows and butterflies. I had to hustle to get business, constantly, because we often seemed to be a heartbeat away from financial ruin. I made rookie mistakes, embarrassing ones; even when I'd done everything right, I experienced rejection after rejection. I had to dust myself off and keep going, though. There was no plan B. My high school diploma wouldn't be a ticket to a better job. I knew that being offered a partnership at Venture was my one big break, my main chance to make enough money to get custody of my children. The company *had* to succeed.

Remembering all this as I lay in bed with the blinds closed, flattened by post-flood exhaustion and despair, I had a startling, almost visceral memory of my own hunger and drive during my first years at Venture. Back then, there was no such thing as being too tired. I'd stay up all night reworking presentations, photocopying, and stuffing envelopes until my fingers were covered in paper cuts.

And then there were the cold calls. I hadn't had to make one in decades, but the memory was as clear as though I'd just hung up the phone (or been hung up on, which did happen). Whenever I heard a company was interviewing other marketing agencies, I used to call and ask to speak to someone in the marketing department. This was pre-Internet, so I couldn't google any names and figure out whom to ask for, which often meant I wound up trying to sweet-talk a secretary who didn't suffer fools gladly. I'd say: "My name is Arlene Dickinson. I'm with a company called Venture. I hear you're doing an agency review and we'd like to come in and pitch." The person on the other end of the line never said, "Fantastic! How soon can you get over here?" Usually, the recipients of these calls would reel off a laundry list of reasons why it would be a cold day in hell before they'd listen to a pitch from the likes of us. They'd already selected the short list. They'd never heard of us. The person who decided which agencies got to pitch was tied up in a meeting and wasn't expected to be free again for, oh, six or seven months. And so on.

At first, I used to apologize for wasting their time and end the call as fast as I could, feeling about an inch tall. I learned to keep pushing (politely—pushing, not pushy). "Well," I'd say, "I hear you. But all I'm asking for is an hour of your time. You'll hear some new ideas, and then we'll be out of your hair. What have you got to lose?" Once in a while it worked, and we'd get a foot in the door. And then we'd work our tails off to come up with a solid pitch, which we'd rehearse and rehearse and rehearse. Doing the work built my confidence and made me feel I had a right to be in the room. Venture was always the dark horse in the running, but eventually we won our first big client, which instantly elevated our reputation. The relief and exhilaration were like nothing I'd ever experienced. We were on our way, and I had had something to do with that.

Ten years in, when I really began to feel I had the hang of things, I took on a whole new set of challenges by buying out my partners and becoming sole owner of Venture. I had an ambitious vision: to expand the company and go toe to toe with the big firms in Toronto and Montreal. That was another wild ride, and one that ensured humility; I learned how to grow a business by trial and error (errors, to be completely accurate). I also learned what the Canadian "no" means, and how to counter it. I was told we were too small and, later, as we grew, that we were too big. It took me a while to recognize that when someone tells you you're not the right size or the right whatever, it's just another way of saying that you're not a good fit—and that's a golden opportunity for you to persuade them that, in fact, you could be. Too small? "We'll scale." Too big? "We're entrepreneurial." Figuring out how to be the right fit became the key to our success.

As the years passed, Venture started to become the company I'd dreamed it could be. We opened an office in Toronto. We landed major national and multinational clients. We won "best managed business" awards. By 2007 or so, we were no longer the upstart trying to elbow our way into the party. We'd arrived.

Wasn't that what we'd been striving for all along? Yes. But retracing our history, I could suddenly see what hadn't been at all obvious at the time: as soon as we started to succeed, we were in danger. Canadian economist Danny Miller has a theory that success is a double-edged sword for many companies. Organizations that flourish can wither and die abruptly when their strengths and business victories make them overly confident. Miller calls it the Icarus Paradox, after the figure in Greek mythology who plummets to his death when he flies too close to the sun and his waxen wings melt. Similarly, high-flying companies can quickly become complacent, switching over to autopilot at the very moment they should start trying to navigate new territory.

This is probably the reason that so few companies last more than a decade or two: they experience success then stop innovating and try to coast. But longevity doesn't happen without innovation and reinvention. "Traditional business" is an oxymoron, when you think about it.

In retrospect, it's clear that success was particularly dangerous for Venture, because our brand was all about being the outsider who tried harder. Once we had a seat at the table, we lost a big part of what had made us unique. We started to be like everyone else.

At the time, of course, this didn't seem like cause for worry, because Venture had never been on such solid ground. These were our glory days! We had great clients, ones that any agency would love to have on its roster, and higher visibility than ever before. The company was in such good shape that I felt I could step back from it and focus on new challenges, such as appearing on *Dragons' Den*. I hired other people to manage Venture from day to day, but although they were qualified and competent, they tended to focus on keeping the company chugging along the same track it was already on. Without a sense of our proudly independent, entrepreneurial roots, they felt no urgency to try to return to them. Nor did I, I must admit. I was so distracted by everything else I was doing that I figured we could just keep going in the same direction indefinitely. In hindsight, however, the peril we were in is obvious: once the company lost touch with its outsider identity, we started to lose our way. Just like Icarus.

Revisiting our history was one of the most productive steps I took on the road to reinventing the company. It helped me under-stand the chain of events that had endangered Venture long before muddy flood water poured into our office building. Crucially, looking back helped me zero in on our core values—and also made it clear how far we'd strayed from them. We had started life as a scrappy, independent agency that marched to the beat of our own drum; we'd instinctively sided with underdogs, because that's how we saw ourselves too. Although the path forward wasn't yet clear, by looking backwards, I'd found the key to our reinvention: we had to find a way to reclaim our identity.

Is this your history, or historical fiction?

Your history, your patterns of behaviour—you need a really firm grasp of both in order to pivot and find a new direction. Otherwise, it's almost guaranteed that your reinvention will falter. You may already have discovered this first-hand. Maybe you left an unhappy relationship and shortly thereafter bounced right into a relationship that seemed wonderful—at first. But then that relationship too sputtered out. The issue probably wasn't "not being ready" for another relationship (let's face it: anyone who's been in a bad relationship is definitely ready for a good one!). More likely, you got yourself into a new version of the same old mess because you didn't know yourself well enough to know what you wanted and needed from another person. Or perhaps you've exchanged one job, or house, or city for another, expecting happiness and fulfillment to follow, but soon found yourself having all the same feelings that drove you to seek a change in the first place.

A lot of people repeat the same patterns over and over because they don't even recognize that's what they're doing. You can't, unless you really know yourself—the true, warts-and-all version, not the idealized cyber-self who exists only on your Facebook page—and understand your history.

Figuring out who you used to be isn't a waste of time, nor is it self-indulgent; if it were, there's no way profit-driven corporations would do it as a matter of course when they're trying to determine next steps. You need an accurate understanding of your history for the same reasons they do: seeing your past clearly, through a lens that's not blurry or distorted, reminds you of your own core values and unlocks your sense of your own possibilities.

As in the corporate world, this won't be a sentimental journey. It's a fact-finding mission, and the purpose is wholly practical. You're looking for signposts that point the way to a new direction in life, just as I found clear indicators of our future direction by revisiting Venture's past.

Outside of a therapist's office, many people don't think analytically about their own past so much as trot out a pat narrative about it. I'm talking about the stories you tell yourself and other people about the key events and turning points, as well as the character strengths and fatal flaws, that made you who you are today. "My parents took me to Ottawa when I was a kid, and that was it: I knew I'd go into politics." "I was going to go to Japan and teach English for a year, I had my ticket and everything, but then I found out I was pregnant. It changed my whole life." "I'm shy and I'm not good at schmoozing, which is why I'm always passed over for management positions, no matter how hard I work."

Your narrative can acquire the status of irrefutable truth in your own mind, as though it's been engraved on a stone tablet and handed down from on high, but there's nothing objective about it. It's a subjective interpretation of your past, often created long after the fact. The purpose of these stories is to make sense of what's happened to us and assign a meaning to it, but not infrequently we unintentionally omit facts, embellish extensively or draw wild conclusions. Your "history" may, in fact, be historical fiction.

Think back to a time when you've argued with someone else's version of a story. It can be infuriating how firmly someone will stick to her guns, even when you know for a fact that she's dead wrong. Sometimes your versions of events are so different that it's as though they took place in parallel universes. "No, it wasn't May, it was July. Remember, it was just after Canada Day? And it wasn't Mark who took the boat—he wasn't even there! It was *Greg*. I know for sure it was Greg because he was wearing that stupid Hawaiian shirt when he pulled back from the dock and crashed into the rocks, and I remember thinking, 'No one who wears a shirt like that should be allowed to drive a boat.' How can you not remember this?"

There's a strong possibility that some of your own stories about yourself are equally skewed and inaccurate. And that's significant, because these stories aren't just about the past—they also influence the future, and what you believe is possible. Think about it: if the moral of the story you tell about yourself is that you're a loser who will never amount to much, guess what? You're not likely to amount to much. You probably won't even try. But if your central theme is that you've had some tough breaks but soldiered on, you're likely to believe that a happy ending is just around the next bend, and you'll keep going until you get there.

Your story about yourself can put you in a box or take you out of one. Regardless, the way you frame your past may blind you to the signposts you're looking for now, the ones that suggest a new path you could take. So for now, forget your narrative. Forget the anecdotes you've told so many times that everyone who knows you could recite them in their sleep. Forget "why" something happened, who's to blame, what it proves about you and what it says about the world in general. A brief spell of amnesia would be helpful, but, failing that, think of yourself as a detective, an objective and impartial one, who's sifting through history looking for clues to the future. You're trying to remember who you were deep inside, before you got cynical and before your inner critic learned how to push your buttons.

Just as we do a deep dive on our clients' companies by rifling through their records and papers, you can dig through your own memorabilia: photo albums, yearbooks, report cards, old journals, school projects, and, if you're a certain age, cards and letters—anything that will take you back, way back, and remind you who you used to be. Attitude is everything here. You're not misty-eyed, wallowing in nostalgia. You're detached, curious and open-minded, the way you would be if you were poking through a box of some stranger's stuff that you found in your attic. What sort of kid were you? Sunny or serious? Dreamy or determined? Competitive or shy? What kinds of things did you like to do, and why? What inspired you, and whom did you admire? What moved you, and what excited you? What did you want to be when you grew up, and why? Take notes, if it helps.

If you're drawing a blank, or if you feel no connection what-soever to the kid with the regrettable haircut in the yearbook picture, you might want to ask people who knew you well when you were younger, "What was I like? What do you remember about me?" Even friends from elementary school are pretty easy to locate via the Internet, and if you haven't seen or heard from them in years, their memories are like something out of a time capsule: untouched by the passing years, or by knowledge of what you've done with your life. A friend of mine who remembered herself as an awkward, withdrawn wallflower of a kid was shocked to be told by a former classmate, "Oh, you were the bold one, always had your hand up in class to ask why. And you were always campaigning for some cause, like preventing cruelty to animals or putting a vending machine in the cafeteria." It was all true, but my friend had edited it right out of her own narrative about herself.

You may be wondering why it even matters—what's passed is past. Only it isn't. Your narrative about the past shapes how you feel about yourself today and what you think you're capable of in the future. When you fact-check your own stories and fill in the blanks, you gain an alternate version of your history, a different idea of your own capabilities and a much better sense of the patterns of your life thus far.

In the same way that going back to first principles often revitalizes a company, revisiting your childhood self puts you directly in touch with your own optimistic, open-to-all-the-universe-has-to-offer self. You'll probably notice aspects of yourself that you'd forgotten, or that had never even occurred to you before: interests, values, passions, convictions and character traits that change not just your view of the past but also your sense of what's possible in the future. If you discover that you've lost your way or sold yourself short, don't freak out. It's not too late to chart a course that allows you to be true to your best self. You just needed to remind yourself who that is.

Hunting for seeds

Full disclosure: reluctant as I was to review Venture's history, I was even more reluctant to revisit my own. I always feel antsy when other people start reminiscing about the old days, and try to steer the conversation back to the present (or, better yet, the future) as fast as I can. Looking forward, there's so much hope and possibility; mistakes have yet to be made. The future is limitless. The past is limiting.

And there's something else. I've survived more than a few traumatic events over the years, as a kid from a dysfunctional family, and I don't think of them as the good old days. I always felt different from the other kids at school, and in some important respects I was. I was two years younger than everyone else because I'd started school early and then had skipped ahead, so I was the scrawny, short one in the class picture. And although in my family there was an unspoken agreement to try to pass as Canadians after we emigrated from South Africa—my mom and dad never spoke Afrikaans in public, only privately, to one another, at home—we didn't fool anyone. My parents had "weird" accents and, initially, no real concept of "winter." One day my mother tucked a worn silk scarf from the Salvation Army around my head and sent me over to the park to go tobogganing in the snow. It didn't cross anyone's mind that a hat and gloves might be a good idea.

We were also different because there wasn't a lot of money, to say the least. I remember being excited to go to the grocery store in the same way that another kid might be excited to go to a toy store. It was a big event, not a regular occurrence. For Sunday dinner, we might bake up a bag of McCain french fries with ketchup, and if we were really lucky, we'd have sour cream too. If I somehow got my hands on a dollar, I would walk to the Safeway to buy plums or raspberries. In a home where food was canned or boxed, fresh fruit was a luxury. Once, a classmate who'd come over to play made fun of me at school the next day because I'd offered her guava juice (standard in South Africa) and an avocado. This was doubly devastating because I'd proudly presented her with that avocado, as it was such a rare treat.

Reflecting on my childhood, it was striking to me how many of my memories involved feeling like an outsider. As a kid, my awareness that I was different had been painful, and my narrative about the past was accompanied by a sad soundtrack, full of wistfully sighing violins. But I realized something important about myself when I reviewed my past objectively (well, as objectively as I could).

There was another way to tell my story: being different has been my ticket. It was why I'd been successful at Venture; I was an outsider to the world of marketing, and I'd knocked myself out to prove that I could do it. Later, as the female CEO of a Calgary-based independent agency, I'd been an anomaly in Toronto, which was a plus. People noticed us. And being different is definitely why I was asked to audition for *Dragons' Den*. This was in 2007, the show's second season. All the other Dragons were male, and my company wasn't worth as much as some of theirs, nor was I as flashy a mogul, nor was my style as combative —all pluses, in the producers' eyes, because it meant I'd add another dimension to the show.

Being different, too, meant that once I joined the show, I was pretty visible, virtually overnight. When the mantle of "female role model" was placed on my shoulders, the weight of it was startling and I felt totally unworthy. I was still trying to figure out my own life—how on earth could I possibly be a good example for anyone else?! But then women started coming up to me on the street, in the supermarket, at the hairdresser's, telling me about their own business ideas and how afraid they'd been to act on them until they'd seen that you don't have to have an MBA, or come from money, or be part of the boys' club, or be a thirty-year-old tech whiz to get somewhere. I realized that being a role model doesn't mean being perfect—in fact, it was my imperfection, and all the ways I was different from most CEOs, that seemed to give other people confidence. *If she can do it, maybe I can too.*

And there it was, one of the seeds of my reinvention: sifting through my past looking for patterns, I realized that I must *need* to feel like an outsider, because I've sought out the role again and again. It's actually my sweet spot. It's a key part of my identity, part of who I've been since as far back as I can remember. I wasn't proud of being different when I was a kid, but as an adult I can't imagine wanting to conform. I'm not comfortable taking the conventional route or doing things the usual way. It's just not me. No wonder I'd felt so restless once Venture morphed from perpetual upstart into a more traditional marketing agency. Being a traditional CEO of a traditional company just isn't who I am. No wonder we'd run into trouble. I just wasn't cut out for the mainstream.

Whatever I did next, I knew it had to be something unconventional, something that allowed me to be an outsider again. I realized, too, that one reason it took me so long to understand that Venture was in danger of stalling was that *I* hadn't stalled—I was focused on yet another uphill struggle. I'd been a behind-the-scenes marketer my whole life, so suddenly finding myself centre stage on a reality TV show was truly bizarre, especially since I hadn't ever imagined being on television and hadn't sought out the role. Rather, the showrunners asked me to audition, and I did, as a lark more than anything else. After I got the part, the learning curve was steep and multi-faceted. I had to learn how to feel comfortable in front of the camera, how to be sure I was heard when the other Dragons talked over me, how to deal with public attention, how to invest in young companies and mentor entrepreneurs. I had my hands full, in the same way I'd had my hands full in the early days of Venture. (This is an explanation, not an excuse: I'd become a distracted CEO. If I wanted to save the company, that couldn't happen again.)

So here was another seed: I recognized that I need to be learning and taking on new challenges in order to feel fully engaged. Otherwise, I tend to check out. There's something about stretching for a goal, and not being sure if I'll actually make it, that I feed off and enjoy. In terms of my reinvention, this meant that I'd have to change Venture in some fundamental way and try to do something really new with it—both for the health of the company and to satisfy my own weird need for uphill battles.

One more thing I noticed, looking back at mini-me: food has always been a major theme in my life. My memories of going to the grocery store with my mother, or of biting into a ripe plum, are way more vivid and detailed than any recollection I have of being in a classroom. Knowing what it is to feel hungry is why, for years, I was a spokesperson for the Breakfast Club of Canada, which helps get a good solid meal to some of the one in five Canadian school kids who don't have anything at home to eat for breakfast.

My interest in food goes beyond wanting to be sure other people have enough, though. I love cooking and, yes, eating. One of my main goals when I got married (at nineteen!) was to be a great cook and a thrifty one. I baked bread and canned vegetables to save money, and I obsessed over making perfect cakes and pies. Thinking about this, I remembered something I'd forgotten for at least thirty years: in my twenties, I came up with an idea for a new kind of pie tin. It used to bother me that the crimped edges of my pies would sometimes burn. What if disposable pie tins were manufactured with an extra piece of tinfoil all around them, which you could fold over the edges of your crust to protect them from burning? This was a genius concept, in my opinion, and I researched how to manufacture it and what it would cost. But this was a time when you couldn't just call up a factory in China and say, "I want to make this thing, please help." My idea (which wasn't so genius, really) went nowhere.

But on *Dragons' Den*, I was often drawn to entrepreneurs pitching similar gadgets or new food products. I viewed their companies as good investments or I wouldn't have bought in, but these entrepreneurs also interested and engaged me on a deep level that had nothing to do with business acumen and everything to do with a passion that has been with me since I was a little kid. I saw myself in them, and I loved being able to experience, albeit vicariously, the thrill ride of starting a food company.

I was particularly interested in the connection between food and health, which was a passion of my father's too, especially after he was diagnosed with cancer. He became really interested in the relationship between what he ate and how he felt, and got me interested in it as well. Sadly, I discovered that the pies and cakes I loved to bake tasted great at the time but made me feel not so great later on.

So I'd found the third seed of my reinvention: I wanted to do something with food. Going from marketing to food is not exactly an obvious step. It was one that probably wouldn't have crossed my mind unless I'd really spent some time immersed in the past, thinking about the person I used to be—and apparently still am, in terms of my core interests, needs and sense of purpose.

I wasn't sure exactly how to translate the excitement I'd felt as a kid, walking into Safeway with a handful of quarters, into a new path for myself. But I knew I wanted to try.

Looking for the patterns in my own history gave me a really good sense of the ways I wanted to try to change my life: I needed to find a real challenge, one that would put me outside the mainstream, and I wanted it to have something to do with food. These were the seeds of my reinvention. Now for the hard part: figuring out where, when and how to plant them so that they'd take root.

Self-awareness is the secret sauce of reinvention

We've all met those magpie types who grab whatever's in front of them, willy-nilly. I've seen it among some very smart people: "Oh, gold's the big thing now? I'm getting into gold." "Restaurants are hot? I'm in." These people are opportunists, not reinventors. Sometimes they have such deep pockets that by the time one endeavour falls apart, they're already on to the next thing. But let's be clear: they're not reinventing—they're flitting, blown about by greed or whatever wind is prevailing at the moment. They react rather than reinvent, because they don't really know who they are.

Once you've done the work of identifying the enduring themes of your life, even if you haven't found the seeds of your reinvention, you'll already know yourself better than you did before. And the more tuned in you are to what you value and what you need in order to be happy, the more you will be able to trust your intuition instead of fumbling blindly for the next big thing.

Reinvention starts with you, and your own understanding of yourself. Nobody else can do it for you, because nobody else knows your core values or the themes of your life, much less what you're capable of and who you aspire to be. Charting a brand new course isn't about chasing down the next hot thing or grabbing on to someone else's coattails and trying to hitch a ride to a better future. Reinvention is about figuring out who you have always been, and how you can use what you already have to become who you want to be. It's not just "There it is!"—with eyes focused on the horizon. It's also "Here I am"—eyes inward.

Chapter 4

On purpose

Purpose has become an incredibly important concept in marketing, one that's changed both how corporations conduct themselves and how consumers evaluate them. In a nutshell, purpose is "a higher order reason for a brand to exist than just making a profit," in the words of Simon Sinek, a former adman turned leadership guru. His TED Talk on the subject has been viewed many millions of times, and caused more than one CEO to pick up the phone and call me to say, "Help! I need to figure out what our purpose is."

Sinek's view is that every organization on earth knows *what* it does: sells stuff. Some even know *how* they do it: what differentiates them from competitors. But very few know *why*. The "why" is not making money—that's an outcome. Rather, it's the reason the company exists in the first place. Its purpose for being. That could be "to accelerate the world's transition to sustainable energy"

(Tesla). Or "to celebrate every woman's unique beauty" (Dove). But if an organization doesn't know what its purpose is, it won't achieve its full potential.

Purpose-driven companies have a significant edge over their competitors, for several reasons. First, people want to work for organizations that are making the world a better place—especially millennials. More than 60 percent of recent graduates factor a company's commitment to sustainability into their decision when they're choosing between jobs, according to a Deloitte survey. And people work harder for purpose-driven companies: 90 percent of employees in these kinds of companies report feeling engaged in their work, compared with just 32 percent of employees in other companies.

Second, consumers want to buy stuff from these kinds of companies. In survey after survey, large majorities of people say that corporations should play a role in improving society, not just focus on making money. Buying patterns have shifted as a result. Increasingly, we give our business only to companies that share our values, whether that's being environmentally conscious, or promoting diversity, or treating labourers fairly.

Third, and this is connected to the first two, purpose-driven companies are much more successful. In a ten-year study of fifty thousand brands conducted by Jim Stengel, the former chief marketing officer of Procter & Gamble, the top fifty performers were purpose-driven brands, and they grew three times as fast as their competitors.

This confirms something I've always felt intuitively: you don't have to choose between purpose and profit. In fact, purpose generates profit. That's at least in part because purpose also generates consistency, which, again, is key to the strength of a brand. A sense of purpose acts like a compass to guide a company in every decision, large and small, so that everything from its corporate culture to its packaging is consistent. Companies that don't just talk the talk but also walk the walk have exceptionally strong brands.

Every time a company hires us, therefore, we're looking to uncover their sense of purpose, or help to create one. Some already operate with a strong sense of purpose—they're just not sure exactly how to articulate it. For example, Dr. Alan Ulsifer, the founder of FYidoctors, came to us with a remarkable success story. An optometrist who trained at the University of Waterloo, he'd banded together with a few like-minded eye doctors in 2008; today, FYidoctors is Canada's largest doctor-owned eye care provider.

Dr. Ulsifer walked us through the benefits of consolidation, explaining that individual optometrists can't afford the latest and greatest equipment, and they have to spend a lot of time dealing with administrivia. By joining forces and consolidating, optometrists get access to state-of-the-art technology for eye exams, and a lot of administrative headaches go away because everything is centralized; since they're group buying, they also get better prices and have access to a greater selection of glasses frames and other tools of the trade. And while a lot of optometrists have to rely on cheap lenses from China, those who belong to FYi get their lenses from the company's own lab in British Columbia, where they use cutting-edge technology and premium materials, so the lenses are extremely high quality.

Dr. Ulsifer is a typically low-key Westerner, but he was visibly proud of the company he'd built: the doctors were top-notch and the equipment was cutting-edge, therefore the eye exams were state of the art, as were their Canadian-made lenses. So what was the company's purpose? Once we really understood their business, it was obvious. A big conglomerate might have an optometrist in its stores to perform eye exams, but its business model is all about selling as many glasses as possible. FYi's business model is all about enhancing patients' lives.

It's nice that they have the best tools and the best lenses and they can spend more time with patients because they don't have to worry about administrative stuff, but those are just the *how*: how they deliver eye care. The *why* was what really made the company different: it's owned by doctors, and what doctors care about most is the health of their patients. The reason they get out of bed every morning is not to sell glasses (though they do that too) but to make their patients' lives better. FYi has a program to provide eye care and glasses for underprivileged Canadian kids not because it makes the company look good, but because they're eye doctors, and they can't stand the thought of little kids not being able to see the blackboard just because their parents don't have a lot of money.

FYi had all the proof in the world that their company is purpose-driven; they just hadn't known how to express what their purpose is. Now that they do, it will help keep the brand on track and consistent—and poised for even greater growth.

Finding a new "why"

Post-flood, we had a different kind of issue at Venture. I'd already bought in to the necessity of reinvention, 100 percent. But we'd lost a lot of people, and a couple of them had set up their own shops and persuaded others to join them. At first, I'd felt personally betrayed when Venture staffers were poached by other former members of our team, but then I started asking myself what I'd done wrong that they didn't stay. It was the right question: how could I make people choose to stay? I wasn't sure that telling the team members who were left that we were going to reinvent the company would do the trick. The prospect of yet more upheaval might only drive more of them away.

I knew, too, that sometimes, when I think I'm just being direct, the team thinks I'm being, well, a bit of a dragon. Once, I told someone, "This is a bad brief," and sent her back to rework it. I'd forgotten all about the incident when, a week later, a senior person pulled me aside to tell me that the woman was still very upset. When I'd said, "The brief is bad," she'd heard, "Your work is bad, and so are you." She might even have feared for her job. That was an important moment for me, a reminder of the importance of self-awareness. My job as CEO is to set the vision for the company and then create the conditions that bring out the best in everyone who works there. I don't ever want to hurt the people who work with me or make them feel devalued.

So when I pulled the remaining senior staff together in the half-finished new office space we'd hastily acquired after the flood, I was nervous. I didn't want to come off as a tyrant and I didn't want to scare people, but I needed everyone to buy in to the idea of reinvention, then and there. We were hemorrhaging money and I'd already concluded, extremely reluctantly, that I would have to close the Toronto office and lay off our people there in order to try to save the jobs of the people now looking at me expectantly. Surrounded by rolled-up carpets and dangling wires, I announced in what I hoped was a strong and positive tone that it was time for a rebirth.

Everyone was very quiet. The frowny, skeptical expressions on the faces around the table weren't encouraging.

Nevertheless, with a marker and whiteboard, we set about doing the kind of audit we perform for other companies. We reviewed our history, the highlights and lowlights, and went over the ways the agency had faltered after the flood—and before. We looked critically at our own process and practices, asking, "Why do we do it that way?" If the only answer was "Because we always have," we knew that was probably something we had to change.

The real turning point came when we began to enumerate our strengths and weaknesses. We were never the data and analytics whizzes. We didn't have huge media buying power. What we were really good at was coming up with marketing strategies and great creative work. And we were strongest strategically, and most passionate personally, when working with entrepreneurial companies like FYidoctors.

Working with upstarts and outsiders was, of course, part of the agency's DNA. Way back when, it's how we'd got our start. And through my work on *Dragons' Den* as well as the creation of youinc.com, the digital platform we'd created for entrepreneurs who were just getting going, we had a tremendous amount of experience with entrepreneurial businesses. We championed these companies not just because we were paid to but because we'd drunk the Kool-Aid: entrepreneurial businesses are the ones that will lift the Canadian economy.

A ripple of excitement in the room. We'd found our new purpose: supporting Canadian entrepreneurs. Everything we did going forward had to serve that purpose.

Have you ever driven, white-knuckled, through fog? It's really stressful because you can't see what's up ahead and you're fearing imminent disaster; but then, all of a sudden, your car pushes through and the fog vanishes and you can see clearly what's been there all along. That's what it felt like, fumbling through our present distress, searching for clues to the future. When our purpose emerged, it was like a burst of sunshine revealing the path forward.

For the first time since the flood, I felt energized and even a little hopeful. Working with entrepreneurs was what had pulled me away from Venture in the first place, so the prospect of focusing solely on entrepreneurial businesses made my heart beat a little faster, in a good way. I also knew what a difference we could make. Most new businesses start as pretty lean operations, and they don't have in-house marketing capability or chief marketing officers, the way major corporations do. For many, marketing is an afterthought. But it's absolutely critical to growth, especially in sectors like consumer packaged goods. You can have the greatest product since sliced bread, but if no one knows about it, it's . . . toast.

In subsequent staff meetings where we started to develop the strategy that would help us pivot, everyone else seemed gung-ho too. But afterwards, privately, there was pushback. People started coming to me individually to voice their concerns, which went something like this: "Small businesses have small budgets, so we won't get big, meaty projects and we won't have the opportunity to do national work anymore. My job will be less interesting and fulfilling, and you'll have a hard time attracting the kind of talent we need in order to rebuild."

There was a lot of fear, but it was based on a fundamental misunderstanding: people were confusing entrepreneurs with small business owners. They are not one and the same. An entrepreneur sees an opportunity to do something that no one has ever done before, and wants to build it from scratch and scale it significantly; a small business owner wants to buy a franchise, say, or open a dry cleaning business, not invent a whole new way to do something. Both have a greater appetite for risk than most people—they're prepared to forgo a steady paycheque, for one thing—but entrepreneurs want to disrupt an industry, the way Uber and Airbnb did, by doing something in an entirely new way. Small business owners aren't trying to take the world by storm; mostly, they want to work for themselves and feel they're in control of their own livelihood and destiny.

I kept having to explain the difference, and say, "Let's talk about WestJet or Cirque du Soleil—companies started by entrepreneurs who had big dreams and visions of changing or disrupting their industries. Sure, they're massive now, but they still do business in a distinctly entrepreneurial way. We're going to focus on *those* kinds of clients, not small business owners."

At one point, I'd given the same spiel so many times that I really started to wonder if my communication skills had deteriorated, or if my team was a little less brilliant than I'd always thought. So I slowed down and really listened to them, instead of reeling off definitions and examples. And I realized something: the person who'd created the confusion was me. All along I'd been calling myself an entrepreneur, and it was certainly true that I had an entrepreneurial mindset and was comfortable taking risks. But I'd never disrupted an industry or built an empire or tried to change the world by inventing a whole new way to do something. In truth, I was more like a very ambitious small business owner.

What I really wanted to be, though, was an entrepreneur. To become one, I'd have to reinvent more than my company. I'd also have to reinvent myself—not just my professional self, but *me*.

Knowing your *why*

In the months after the flood, I couldn't have told you what my own personal dreams and aspirations were. I was just trying to get through each day. During that dark time, I dragged myself to a meeting at the bank to figure out my next move. Exhausted, I sat across from my banker and told him that I was going to put more of my own money into Venture to buy more time. He seemed both genuinely concerned about me and convinced that I'd lost my marbles. Looking at me incredulously, he asked why on earth I would that.

I really had to think about it. Why *was* I doing it? He was right that it would be easier, in many ways, just to close the business down than to try to reinvent it. There were times when I yearned to be free of the constant anxiety and guilt, just shrug it all off, hang up a "going out of business" sign and be done with it. But I couldn't. It wasn't pride that kept me going—I'd had to swallow what was left of that months before. It was my team. They had mortgages, car payments, kids to feed and, in all likelihood, spouses who were urging them to jump ship before we sank. But they hadn't bailed. That was both a source of comfort and a heavy responsibility. I felt that I'd let them down once already. I wasn't going to do it again.

There was another reason to try to keep the business afloat too. Venture's new core purpose, supporting entrepreneurs, was also *my* core purpose. And I knew I had a better shot at fulfilling it with a large organization behind me. Standing solo on the sidelines, playing fairy godmother, your impact is limited. You can help a handful of people, max. I wanted to do better than that.

Growing up, it was deeply ingrained in me that if you help other people, that's a win for you too, and that's certainly been my

experience. Nothing I've done in my career has been as rewarding as funding fledgling companies and mentoring newly minted
entrepreneurs. I don't mean financially rewarding—profit is just an
outcome, and a pretty uncertain one with very young companies,
because the failure rate is high. I'm talking about the fulfillment
that comes along with helping someone else try to turn a good
idea into a viable business. Especially if that someone else reminds
me a little of myself: tentative but willing to work hard, with big
dreams and a soft heart. Sometimes I had the uncanny feeling
that I was reaching back through time and lending a helping hand
to my younger self, the one who got all excited about pie tins and
thought that gift baskets were the ticket to success. That made
me feel good, and it also felt like something I owed the universe:
payback for all my good fortune.

I wanted to help more of those very early stage entrepreneurs,
the true underdogs, but what I'd told the team was true: Venture
would focus only on those whose companies had already taken
flight, like Dr. Ulsifer and FYidoctors. Those companies need
(and can afford) the kinds of complex strategic and branding work
that a full-service agency provides. Seed-stage companies don't
(and couldn't afford it even if they did). What they need is . . .
everything else.

My experience with *Dragons' Den* really solidified for me that
when a good idea doesn't go anywhere, it's usually not because
it isn't good enough. The reason is almost always that the entrepreneurs needed more support, and a different kind of support,
than they'd received. It's damn hard to get both funding *and*
the marketing expertise that's required to get a new product or
service noticed. That was my pitch when guests on the show were
choosing between multiple Dragon offers, and it was something

unique I brought to the table: I could help with both funding and marketing. And I absolutely loved doing it.

Sometimes, though, even funding and marketing help aren't enough. Some entrepreneurs have such big or complex ideas that in order to refine them, they need hands-on mentoring, office space, and access to expensive equipment and administrative support—the kinds of wraparound support that incubators and accelerators provide to seed-stage tech companies. Most of the entrepreneurs who came on the show, though, didn't qualify for those kinds of programs. They weren't in the tech industry, for starters. For a lot of the food and health companies I invested in, there just wasn't anywhere to go to get that kind of guidance and support. I'd seen a few fail, and others never reach their full potential, for lack of it.

I wanted to figure out a way to support those entrepreneurs whose companies were too small for Venture to help—*really* support them, I mean, so that they had the best possible shot at success. So my purpose was to support very early stage companies while somehow simultaneously becoming a bona fide, industry-disrupting entrepreneur myself. And, oh yeah, turn Venture around while I was at it.

Maybe the banker was right, and I really was losing it.

Inspiration is all around

Right around this time, in the winter of 2013, I participated in a charity event in which executives sleep on the streets of downtown Toronto to raise money for Covenant House, a shelter for homeless youth. Along with about twenty others, I was given a sleeping bag and a piece of cardboard and taken to a secure parking lot for the night. Of course, I realize that sleeping in a safe area, in a clean, warm sleeping bag, is nowhere close to the reality of life on the streets, but what I experienced that night changed me.

It may seem obvious, but I was shocked by just how difficult it is to sleep outside for even a few minutes. We were besieged by sudden sounds and strange smells. There was a kind of sensory overload as the city lights and noises seeped into my head at every moment, unstoppable. As the night wore on, it grew colder and colder. I had a hat and mittens, luxuries if you're truly homeless, yet I couldn't stop shivering. Even knowing that the parking lot was secure, I felt vulnerable there, in the open air. It was unbearable to think of kids having to do this every single night.

For the first time in a long time, my mind was free of worry and fear about my company, my team and my own future. I was in the moment, sharply aware of both the cement beneath me and my own good fortune—tomorrow night, I'd be back in my own bed. You know how people say that your own problems shrink into insignificance when you meet people who are less fortunate? While that's true, it wasn't what I experienced that evening. Rather, my confidence in my own ability to change my life had grown, because I'd caught a glimmer of how to do it. I'd just had one of the most inspiring experiences of my life.

Before we'd trudged off with our cardboard and sleeping bags, we'd toured Covenant House, a big Gothic building smack dab in the middle of downtown Toronto, with clusters of young people gathered on the steps outside. I had always thought of shelters as temporary way stations—warm bed, hot meal, move on—but I was surprised by how homey it felt inside. Covenant House is designed not only to help kids get off the streets temporarily but also to help them change their lives permanently. There are beds and hot meals, yes, but also clean clothes on offer, an on-site school and a job training program. There's counselling, health care and pastoral care. There are day programs for kids who aren't in residence as well as long-term housing for young people who need extended support. It's an entire ecosystem, a one-stop support system for reinvention, and kids need all of it, not just a piece or two, according to the ones we met.

After a basic meal of sloppy joes and juice, several graduates of the program had told us how they'd used the services and support they received, both from other kids and from the adults who run the programs, to turn their lives around. Before that night, I'd walked by kids sprawled on the sidewalks and thought, *Why aren't you working?* These young men and women answered that unspoken question, explaining what had pushed them into homelessness. Each story was unique, but all were harrowing, and the common thread was abuse. I was ashamed that I'd never really considered that homeless kids might actually feel safer sleeping on the sidewalk than in their own homes.

"Home" and "family" didn't evoke images of comfort to these young men and women, but memories of neglect and abuse, mentally ill and drug-addicted parents, and the trauma of being bullied, demeaned and preyed upon. Growing up, my own family was garden-variety dysfunctional, and I know what a profound impact that has had on me. But my childhood was paradise compared with what these kids had gone through. Yet they'd turned their lives around. One had taken advantage of the education services at the shelter and gone on to earn a master's degree. Another had started cooking in the Covenant House kitchen and was now a successful chef. A boy who had fled his mother's home had ended up singing on a reality TV show; he'd literally found his voice.

As we listened to them talk, there wasn't a dry eye in the house. This was reinvention of the highest order. These kids had found within themselves the courage and confidence to make life changes that most of us can barely fathom. And they were able to do it because they'd received the personal support and the range of services they needed. I've been writing cheques to charities most of my life, but when people are trying to turn their lives around, they need more than money. They need hands-on practical help, guidance and opportunities of the sort Covenant House offers.

I have no expertise helping kids get off the streets, so I'm going to have to stick to writing cheques, volunteering my time, raising awareness and enthusiastically cheering every success. But that evening, it struck me that I *did* have enough expertise to create another kind of ecosystem, one that could change the prospects of entrepreneurs and young companies by giving them everything they need to survive and thrive. Money and marketing help aren't enough; they also need job training, on-site education and mentoring, support from their peers, and access to equipment they couldn't otherwise afford—just as the kids at Covenant House did.

I wasn't sure how I'd create such an ecosystem, but I did know one thing: it was the kind of ambitious, industry-disrupting move a real entrepreneur would make. My core purpose was already guiding me in the right direction, straight toward my reinvention.

Looking forward for purpose

On *Dragons' Den*, we tend to be pitched by two kinds of entrepreneurs: those who are passionate and those who are blindly passionate. The latter variety always make me nervous. I'll never forget one guy who had sold his house and his possessions and put every penny he had into his idea. His entire family—kids and wife—was living in a one-bedroom apartment. He was on the brink of divorce, and he hadn't sold five cents' worth of his gadget. His passion blinded him to the signs that were clearly telling him to pivot to something else.

I'm not sure I've ever met someone with blind passion who also has a strong sense of purpose. It's all about the *what*—getting rich, or getting famous, or getting powerful—and not the *why*. Over and over, the pitches that do best are the ones where passion is aligned with a strong set of values and guided by a singular sense of purpose.

Maybe you don't know yet what your purpose is. That's okay. Some people have a calling—ministers, medical professionals, poets—but most of us have to fumble around a little to figure out what we're meant to do. You've already looked back. Now try looking forward, to perform an exercise inspired by journalist David Brooks: think about your eulogy, not your resumé. Brooks points out that if your resumé is a measure of your success in the market, your eulogy is a measure of your success as a human being. So picture someone who knows you well, standing up at your funeral to give a speech that sums up your life and the difference you made in the world. What do you hope people remember about you after you're gone? What kind of legacy do you want to leave? It's unlikely that you want the first line of your eulogy to be about your money or possessions. What most of us really want to leave behind is evidence that we were good people, and that we strived to, and did, achieve our purpose.

Even people who have had extraordinary success are remembered as much for their human qualities, and their impact on others, as for their worldly achievements. When you think of Steve Jobs, you recall not only his astonishing capacity for innovation but also how he treated his team at Apple (abusively, by many accounts) and his own daughter (for years, he denied paternity despite knowing that she was his child). With John F. Kennedy, we remember both how he inspired the world and how he betrayed his wife, having affair after affair with young women (which today we'd recognize as an abuse of power). Both men undoubtedly had a very clear vision of what they wanted to achieve and how, but I'd be willing to bet that they didn't have as firm a grip on the "why" of their own existence. I very much doubt that JFK was striving to be remembered as the Hound Dog in Chief, or that Jobs would have wanted the Hollywood movie about his life to focus on what an awful human being he was.

So how do you want to be remembered? The answer should point you in the direction of your core purpose, if you don't already know it. If you have a raison d'être, and you're true to it, it will become the wellspring of a life well lived.

In the last days of her life, the mother-in-law of a friend of mine asked for her help: she wanted to write a letter that could be read aloud at her funeral, to reassure people that she felt she'd had a good life, and was at peace with the idea that it was almost over. For my friend, a writer, it was both the most difficult and the most important assignment she'd ever had. She loved her mother-in-law deeply, so being able to do something meaningful for her at the end of her life felt like a rare privilege but also intensified the grief she was already experiencing.

"She's on her deathbed and I'm sitting there bawling, tears all over my notepad, and she says she wants the letter to be about joy," my friend remembers. "She was drifting in and out of consciousness, so I thought, 'Oh, that's the morphine talking.' But then she said in a really strong voice, 'Life is too important to be taken seriously—write that down.' And the letter wound up being about joy, how to experience it and how to spread it, which is an unusual thing to hear about at a funeral, but it was so *her*. She brought sunshine into every room she ever entered, even at the very end. She didn't think she'd had a big life because she was 'just' a secretary, but she had a huge impact wherever she went because she really did spread joy. She achieved her mission."

Worldly achievement is just the *what* or the *how* of most people's lives. If your *why* doesn't spring to mind readily, give it some time, and start trying to be conscious of what moves you, and inspires you, and fulfills you. Unfortunately, a lot of these words have acquired a kind of New Age sheen, so it may feel hokey or hopelessly earnest to say them, even silently, to yourself. But even the most jaded hipster in the world wants to feel inspired, moved and fulfilled, whether he'll admit it out loud or not. To find your own core purpose, you need to be in touch with your passions, convictions, ideals and beliefs. And then you need to honour them, by staying true to yourself.

Authenticity

When I think back on all the Arlenes— the one who baked bread every night to save money on groceries; the one who fidgeted nervously in her chair on the first day of *Dragons' Den*—I sometimes wonder if they'd be recognizable to each other. I think they would, because in each incarnation I've tried my best to operate with honesty and authenticity. My personal beliefs have informed every business decision and investment I've made. In the same way, I believe that your core values should never be adjusted to pull off a reinvention. They should remain firmly anchored to your core purpose.

"Authenticity" has become a bit of a buzzword, which is a little ironic given that we're up to our ears in "fake." We've seen elections influenced by bots. We're inundated with Kardashian-y plastic lips (and other body parts) and one corporate betrayal after another. Who would ever have thought that Volkswagen would lie to its customers? It's no wonder people have lost faith in business leaders. In this climate, being real is a tactical advantage.

To me, authenticity is all about being real and human, not perfect. Humans do make mistakes on occasion. Authenticity is Jennifer Lawrence tripping on the stairs en route to picking up her first Oscar, then grinning goofily—that was the moment she became America's sweetheart, and the most real star in Hollywood. When someone is authentic, there's no hidden agenda, no phony attempts to impress.

Stumbles and missteps are only embarrassing if you let yourself be embarrassed by them. There's nothing inherently embarrassing about making a mistake—we all make them. It's called being human. If you can laugh at yourself instead, you short-circuit shame, never giving it a chance to flourish.

Here's an example. A few months ago I was out for dinner with a group of friends. At the end of the evening, I stepped away to use the washroom and they went to the bar to wait for me. To rejoin them, I had to walk all the way through the crowded room of well-dressed diners, and as I did, I had a weird feeling: people were watching me, and their facial expressions were really odd. I got up to the bar, and one of my friends leaned close to say, "Look behind you." I did, and there it was: about ten feet of toilet paper caught in my pants, trailing across the restaurant and pointing the way back to the bathroom. It could have been a moment of sheer embarrassment, but I decided instantly that if anyone was going to laugh, it should be on my terms. So I posted what happened on Twitter, and people started responding with their own embarrassing stories. What could have been a moment of mortification became a point of connection.

A little while after that incident, a potential client e-mailed to ask, "Can you make my personal brand 'real' like yours? Do your social media thing for me!" To me, that was a truly bizarre request. My "personal brand"—the "me" I put out there on social media and in the world—*is* me. What I say on social media is said by me. Authenticity can't be generated wholesale by a PR firm (faux authenticity is another matter, but people always catch on anyway, so what's the point?). It's who you are.

But I am *not* saying to "just be yourself" at all times. Sharing your deepest anxieties with your colleagues, showing up in sweats for the presentation, dancing a jig in the boardroom—those are displays not of authenticity but of cluelessness. You can be authentic and still understand what's appropriate behaviour in the context at hand.

Think of authenticity as the armour that protects your sense of purpose. Before you get going on implementing sweeping changes, it's a good idea to figure out which lines you won't cross, because compromises and shortcuts will be waiting along the way like land mines. I've experienced those moments of ethical crisis many times in my career. A request to fudge a financial report. A little white lie that might close the deal. By sticking to my values, I've lost some business along the way, without question. But I can live with that. I couldn't have lived with the compromises.

For instance, I've always said that I would never work with tobacco. I can't be part of promoting something that causes such suffering. When Venture was on its knees, I remember asking myself what I'd do if Philip Morris came to me and offered me $100 million worth of business. Would I have the strength to walk away, if the price was the loss of my own company? I was certain that I would, even knowing that a lot of people I care about would have been hurt by the decision. But I knew that I would rather lose Venture than sell my own values down the river.

Your line might be drawn somewhere else entirely. That's okay, so long as it's consistent with your core purpose. Authenticity lies in knowing yourself and declaring, "This is what I'm all about. And this is what I absolutely won't tolerate." If you find your moral compass wavering, consider this: We live in the age of cellphones and viral videos. You need to be willing to defend in public any decision made in private, because "private" no longer means what it used to—and small snippets of moments can be shared, completely out of context, and their meaning can be distorted wildly.

Your purpose is your legacy

Sometimes purpose evolves over time, with age, experience and exposure to the world. That's what happened with me, and also what I observed in the too-short career of the extraordinary Calgary entrepreneur Suzanne West. Over the years our paths would cross, and it was always memorable, because she was electric with intensity, a true force of nature. Incredibly fit, she had muscular arms that looked as if they could hold up the world, and in her philanthropic work and purpose-driven career it seemed as though she was trying to do exactly that. Anyone who knew her was shocked when she died suddenly in 2018 after a brief, brutal battle with a form of brain cancer. Her obituary in the *Globe and Mail* began, "Suzanne West, who worked to reinvent the traditional Canadian oil and gas company . . . has died. She was 52."

As a CEO in her thirties and forties, Suzanne made a bright mark in the energy sector, building and exiting two successful companies. After selling one company to a rival, though, she was disillusioned and on the cusp of walking away from the industry altogether. Then she attended a retreat for entrepreneurs and philanthropists hosted by Virgin Group founder Richard Branson. She came away renewed and ready to create something new, while also making big changes in her life. She described herself as a former Type A personality who had become more mindful and was now motivated by the lofty goal of wanting to "change the world."

So her next company was Imaginea Energy Corp., an oil and gas company committed to sustainability and community. It was a courageous move in a conservative, male-dominated industry, an effort to reinvent the wheel by harnessing technology such as drones and solar panels to prove that hydrocarbons could be produced sustainably. The world-changing ethos carried over to her personal life too: Suzanne launched several charities and brought foster kids into her home. She meditated regularly, telling *Canadian Business* magazine: "I have lots of doing I want to do, but I make sure I have an equal amount of being in my life, because beingness enhances doingness by, like, 10 times. It's amazing. People are trapped in this mental construct that more doing is what's needed. Hey, we need lots of doing. But if you move 10% of your day into being, I can guarantee your *doing* will double."

It takes courage to change your life, challenge conventional business wisdom, and embrace compassion and generosity the way she did. After that life-changing retreat with Richard Branson, every move Suzanne made seemed informed by a sense of purpose. She once said, "I don't even remember the person I used to be."

One of Suzanne's many charitable pursuits was a fundraiser called Steps to End Homelessness, an annual event she launched to raise money for a non-profit called Inn from the Cold, which provides shelter and care for homeless children and their families. Every year, around her birthday, she'd sponsor a climb to a spectacular viewpoint on the peak of Crescent Hill in Calgary. For several years Suzanne, always so athletic, had led a boot camp in that beautiful, forested park.

A few months after she died, on a bright spring day, hundreds of people gathered in the parking lot, readying themselves to make the climb. It was a day of laughter and tears, and approaching the 167-step staircase, the symbolism was inescapable: having a clear purpose in life makes the uphill climbs possible, and ensures your legacy. Suzanne's lives on, because she didn't just know what her *what* and *how* were; she was crystal clear on the *why* too, and it guided every move she made. That made all the difference, both to her personally and to the world she changed.

What kind of legacy do you want to leave?

When thinking about my core purpose, I was also thinking about what I want to spend the next twenty years of my life doing, and what kind of legacy I want to leave.

I knew that marketing, on its own, wasn't it. Don't get me wrong: I am enormously proud of my company, and I know it has made a difference in other people's lives, not just mine. Venture has paid out a fortune in salaries over the years, and bought a lot of houses and cars for the people who've worked there. It's also helped many clients grow their companies. It's created prosperity for quite a few people, and I'm hugely proud of the work we've done together. But I'm realistic, too. If the agency had never existed, the team would have found another place to earn a living, and our clients would have found another marketing firm.

Entrepreneurs, on the other hand, create businesses that are more than just very good versions of what already exists. They change the game. They don't just read the zeitgeist, they shape it. Uber, Airbnb and Spotify are called "disrupters" because they were fast and first, creating the sharing economy before others could even articulate what that was, and they paved the way for a major shift in how we live.

It was a big moment for me when I realized I wasn't an entrepreneur. Yet. But I knew that I would have to become one in order to create the legacy I hoped to leave: that I changed the game for Canadians with good business ideas, so that they could keep our country strong. Sounds grand, doesn't it? But the truth is that preserving what makes Canada the best place in the world to live requires innovative, ambitious, entrepreneurial businesses. Especially as the population ages and demands on our social safety net increase, we need as many great homegrown companies as we can get. They create jobs, and people who have jobs pay taxes, as do corporations. Good intentions alone won't fund our health care system and our social safety net, or ensure that we can afford to welcome refugees and immigrants warmly, or guarantee that we have the means to protect the natural but fragile beauty of our vast country. All of that requires prosperity, and prosperity requires a vibrant business climate. I want to help create that.

For a long time, I was afraid to say any of that aloud. It sounded grandiose and embarrassingly earnest. But thinking about your core purpose and what legacy you want to leave is serious. And you should be ambitious, because what you're really talking about is the meaning of life—your life. I want mine to mean something.

Don't you?

Part Three

HERE AND NOW

Once you're clear on where you've been, it's time to figure out where you stand right now. You may think you already know, but chances are excellent that there are some holes in your self-knowledge. Certainly there were in mine: I honestly believed that I was already an entrepreneur, but actually I was an entrepreneurial CEO—there's a difference.

So how do you assess your current situation? Well, in marketing, we gather as much information as we possibly can from as wide a variety of sources as possible, in order to get an accurate snapshot of a client's business. We interview company insiders as well as outsiders to find out about the culture of the place, how it actually operates, how other people perceive the company—and to see whether any of the above jibes with the organization's core purpose. Frequently, the answer is "not exactly." There are inconsistencies, and that's bad for any brand.

Furthermore, there are usually sizable gaps between a CEO's vision of a company and how the rank and file view it, and also between insiders' and outsiders' perceptions of the place. A big part of our job is to try to figure out where and why those gaps exist, and how to close them. The goal is to get everybody on the same page, so the company can execute on its core purpose and strengthen its brand.

To do that, we need to understand the organization's strengths and weaknesses—its currency in the marketplace. What more could they be doing with what they have? How could their strengths be used to reinforce the organization's core purpose? Is there any chance of eliminating some of the weaknesses?

What does all this have to do with personal reinvention? Everything, as I discovered when I set about adapting the process we use to help businesses to help change my own path. In a funny way, the approach we use may be even more helpful when what you're trying to change is your own life, because it strips away emotion and focuses on facts you can quantify, such as how you're actually spending your time. If you've been sleepwalking through life, or living in a dream world, this is your wake-up call. You're about to have a bracing encounter with reality, via a self-audit, and it may not be pretty.

Self-auditing is where a real-world reinvention deviates from the "I can do anything!" fantasy. You're forced to figure out who you really are, not who you wish you were. There will be time to think outside the box, but this isn't it. You have to get real with yourself first. That comes from taking stock, thoroughly, of your present *reality*. Is your core purpose guiding your decisions—and if not, why not? What's your currency—the unique skills, assets and core competencies that only you can offer?

If you haven't yet identified your core purpose, the reality check you're about to perform will almost certainly help. Concrete goals and a stronger sense of direction may also suggest themselves at this juncture. There's nothing like being in touch with reality, especially if it's not so pleasant, to help you focus on what needs to change, and how.

Chapter 5

Reality check

Clients hire a marketing firm like Venture for one of two reasons: they're trying to build a dream, or they want the pain to stop. Either way, they want to jump-start the company out of some kind of rut. So the next step in our process, after diving into the organization's past to get a sense of its evolution, values and core purpose, is to map the contours of that rut. To do that, we need factual information on the day-to-day reality of the company's operations. We go straight to the source, interviewing a wide range of employees to be sure we're getting an accurate picture. We ask, What's it like to work here? What does this company do well, and not so well? How does your product stack up against competitors'? What's going right, and what's going wrong?

It's very rare that everyone sings from the same song sheet. A CEO might confidently declare, "Our company is all about X, and our product is state of the art." But other senior executives could tell us, "This company stands for Y," while junior employees might say, "This place is totally dysfunctional, and the quality of our product is a joke." When the team isn't along for the ride, it's sometimes because the CEO's vision doesn't resonate with them emotionally; it just doesn't ring true to their own experience. For instance, if the CEO firmly believes "our company is all about products that help families," yet workers are forever being asked to come into the office on weekends, it's understandable that their take might be, "This company doesn't care about people. All that matters is the bottom line, and God help you if you have a family." By the end of these interviews, it's sometimes abundantly clear that there's a large gap between what senior management thinks the company is and what it actually is. The company's core purpose, if it's ever been articulated, is no longer its North Star.

The gap between the idealized version of the company and the actual organization usually gets significantly wider when we move on to canvass what outsiders think of it. We don't pick them at random. We ask senior management to connect us with people who know the company well—clients, suppliers, board members, anyone who's worked with them on joint projects. We're not looking for disgruntled former employees or activist shareholders or anyone else with an axe to grind; we want people who will be objective and helpful, not malicious. Then we interview these outsiders too, promising them anonymity in return for their honest take on what the company is doing right and wrong.

The day we present our findings can be a sobering one for management. The goal is to increase self-awareness, so they understand where the company *really* is versus where they think or hope it is, and sometimes the truth hurts. We're not delivering our own critique; we're really just holding up a mirror to their business, but they may not like or even recognize the reflection they see. This is especially likely to be the case with family businesses and entrepreneurial ventures, where owners have invested so much of their own time, money and energy into building their companies that they can have a really difficult time accepting input from anyone else and may become very defensive about criticism. Sometimes, even when they learn that the staff is so demoralized that half of them are out looking for new jobs, CEOs dig in and double down: "There's nothing wrong with this place that a new logo wouldn't fix!" The likelihood that such a leader will embrace reinvention is just about zero. Some people reject self-awareness; they just don't want to know. They'd rather be right than be successful.

Self-awareness is a key business skill

I recently read a study confirming that there's a direct correlation between self-awareness and financial success. An in-depth look at public companies revealed that companies with leaders who were described as having few blind spots and reliable self-perception (meaning that their assessment of their own strengths and weaknesses lined up with how others saw them) are more profitable. Conversely, companies whose leaders ranked low in self-awareness were less successful. That makes perfect sense to me. Picture a self-aware business person and a posturing, oblivious one. Who would you rather do business with? Yep, me too.

Things have changed a lot since the eighties, when I got my start in the business world. Back then, greed was good, everyone wanted to make a killing on Wall Street, and a model CEO was one who was ruthlessly devoted to driving profits by any means necessary. Companies were far more hierarchical, so management didn't have to be self-aware—they held all the power. Employees who didn't toe the line got the boot. Today, there's an understanding that diversity has a direct and positive impact on the bottom line and, in the #MeToo era, a growing consensus that how you treat people matters, and has economic consequences. Tone-deaf, tyrannical leaders are now the ones being shown the door. If it comes out that management runs roughshod over employees, a company's stock price may take a hit, no matter how awesome its products are.

In other words, self-awareness counts in business in a way it never has before. It's no longer seen as a "soft skill" or a nice extra, but as a must for leaders who care about success.

What this means in real terms is not that self-aware leaders are perfect people, but that they're willing to listen, learn and course-correct. They may blanch when they hear that insiders and outsiders have a less than rosy view of their company and its leadership, but they are prepared to take in the information and act on it.

For instance, when we presented our initial findings to the CEO of a company whose business involved long-haul transportation, he initially batted away criticism of his leadership. "Yeah, I'm tough. But this is a tough industry." Then we read out a quote from a supplier who'd told us, among other things, "This company has a ton of potential, but they're growing too fast and their people aren't being trained right. Some of the guys in the field are sloppy, and everyone knows it." Whoa. Now we had the guy's attention. He demanded to know our source: "It was Bill, right? Sounds like something he'd say. I'll bet a hundred bucks it was Bill." Well, we said, it wasn't just one person who'd raised this concern. One-quarter of the forty-odd people we'd interviewed had said similar things.

You could see the light bulb go on: the CEO didn't agree with the criticism, but he understood that if word was out on the street, he had to pay attention. Perception is reality, and his brand was in trouble. We collectively held our breath at this point. What was he going to do with this knowledge—push back and rail against detractors? If so, we couldn't help him. You can't rebrand unless you're willing to change the company from within, because a brand isn't just what you say in an ad. It's how you do your work, how you interact in the world—who you *are*, basically. And right now, his brand identity was "sloppy and unprofessional" in an industry where safety is of paramount importance. He got it. "We're meeting training standards, but obviously that's not enough," he grumbled. "We'd better nip this in the bud and get everybody retrained." He was ready to accept that he might have some blind spots when it came to his view of his own leadership, and that other people might see his company differently than he did—and might be right. Self-awareness would help him power his company out of the rut and break the bad habits the organization had fallen into as it had grown. Their reinvention had begun.

Where does the time go?

The issue that both companies and individuals have to be concerned about is whether their actual day-to-day activities are aligned with their core values and sense of purpose. A grand mission statement isn't worth anything if your actions contradict it.

Luckily, when what you're looking to reinvent is your own life, you don't need to hire anyone else to conduct interviews or help you figure out what's really going on every day. Coming up with a snapshot of your day-to-day existence is a DIY project. Bear in mind, though, that that snapshot needs to be accurate. This isn't a carefully filtered selfie but more of a candid photo, one that's true to life and possibly not particularly flattering. Taking that snapshot involves a little consciousness-raising about your own habits. You need to figure out which ones have become so automatic that you no longer even think about them or contemplate eliminating them.

For many years, Toyota was a client of Venture's, and they taught us everything we know about the Japanese concept of *kaizen*: the quest for continuous improvement. At Toyota, employees throughout the organization, from the CEO to the janitorial staff, are always on the lookout for little tweaks and changes that could eliminate waste, ramp up efficiency and improve quality. They are constantly self-auditing, with the goal of making the manufacturing process as lean as possible, and *kaizen* is a key pillar of the corporation's success.

The idea is beautifully simple: be conscious of each step you take, and objective about its usefulness, so you can come up with ways to perform that step even better. It's a hyper-rational approach that zaps emotion out of the equation, which makes it ideal for the task at hand: performing a self-audit of your daily life. You're going to hold a mirror up to your own existence, in the same way that Venture holds a mirror up to each client's company.

To see whether there's a gap between what you think you're doing and what you actually are doing, you need to track how you're spending your time. Starting tomorrow, and for the next four to seven days, keep an hour-by-hour inventory of how you spend your time. I know it sounds nitpicky and finicky, but nothing facilitates self-awareness, or keeps you honest, quite like a time audit. You're going to make the invisible elements shaping your daily existence visible.

Using a spreadsheet makes this exercise easier, but whatever method works for you is fine. Just don't base your time audit on the past; it's really difficult to remember what you did from 3:00 to 3:20 last Monday. And yes, it's important to log everything, especially the stuff you're not so proud of. This is kind of like those food diaries that nutritionists tell you to keep: it's a useless exercise unless you're completely truthful, so include all the Web surfing, texting with friends, runs to Starbucks, and that time you fully intended to go to the gym but somehow wound up sprawled on the couch watching Netflix instead.

The mere fact of having to write down what you're doing will make you a lot more conscious of what you're doing with your time, and may help curb any bad habits you've fallen into. But you're not off the hook yet.

Once you've completed the inventory, sort your time into three separate categories. In the first category, include all the hours spent on productive routines, meaning that you actually accomplished something, even if that "something" was just hauling yourself into the office or making sure your kids didn't starve to death or going for a run to lower your stress level. In the second category, count all the hours that were linked to your core purpose, whether that's learning (so, for example, reading a book, researching, attending a lecture would all count), or being a great parent, or whatever purpose you identified in the last chapter. Finally, the third category is for downtime and distractions: hours spent doing things that weren't explicitly productive or didn't move you closer to achieving any goals.

The purpose of this exercise is to identify what you're actually doing with your days, and to help you realize that you have a lot more control over your time than you may think. Check out your routines in category one. Is there a way to speed any of them up, or at least shake them up, so that they become less stressful and more productive? If, for example, you spend your morning commute in the car swearing at other drivers while listening to a Top 40 station, what about switching to an audiobook on a topic you wish you knew more about? Or taking public transit, so you can get through all the e-mails jamming up your phone? Or getting some exercise in—walking or cycling at least part of the way to work? It sounds basic, I know, and it is—so basic that many of us don't bother to implement any of these little *kaizen*-type changes that could fundamentally improve our lives.

Now look at your third category. Downtime isn't all created equal. Some activities leave you feeling relaxed, entertained and refreshed: a walk in the woods, an evening with good friends, an hour in front of the fire with a good book, watching a great movie—whatever it is, it replenishes you. And then there's killing time: frittering away hours on social media, mindlessly surfing the Web, binge-watching shows you can't even remember the next day, playing addictive online games—stuff that leaves you feeling empty, numb and a little guilty. Rate your downtime hours in terms of enjoyment on a scale of one to three. Hours that made you feel great, both while they were happening and afterwards, get threes. Hours that were empty or wasted get ones. Anything in between gets a two.

If your third category is bulging with ones and twos, whatever you're doing may be a form of self-medication to distract yourself from the pain, boredom or disappointment of your own life. But you're deepening whatever rut you're in, too, without addressing the root problem: your time expenditures don't reflect and aren't tied to your core purpose. In a very fundamental way, you're not being true to yourself. If you want to improve your life, start by spending more hours behind door number two, which is all about activities that sync with your core purpose. Even if you shift just an hour or two a week from category three into category two, it will make a real difference in terms of what you're able to accomplish and how you feel about yourself.

The goal here isn't to program every second of your day, but to make you aware of where the time is going so you can begin to make some improvements. Some people reverse-engineer this by creating really rigid schedules for themselves. I have one friend who follows her routine like she's an army of one. She's up at 4 a.m. every single day, even on weekends. She works out. Checks e-mail. Breakfast. The office. Event. Home. Bed. Up at 4 a.m. Rinse and repeat. Every minute of her day is booked, every single day. I tease her about all the coloured blocks on her iCal, but she's happy. Not coincidentally, however, she's been in the same job and relationship for decades. Her schedule keeps her on track, and she's happy with her life, which is fortunate because I don't think she could pull off a reinvention—how could she find the time?

I'm not big on routines, though even I will admit that some habits are worth sticking to: eating well, exercising, always showing up a little early—common-sense stuff that makes your life better. But most habits aren't about improving your life; they're about making you feel safe and comfortable. It's human to want to be comfortable. But as any personal trainer will tell you, if you're comfortable, you're not getting stronger and you're not growing. At best, you're treading water. At worst, comfort induces full-on inertia (see: frittering away hours on social media and binge-watching forgettable TV).

Even "good" habits can be a trap. If your house always has to be spotless, or you're in the habit of obsessively redrafting work e-mails, your habits may give you the illusion of being in control, but in fact you're being controlled by them. They're eating into your time, and probably also limiting your willingness and ability to change.

I don't know anyone who has successfully changed course, either personally or professionally, while stubbornly clinging to old habits. To change your life, you have to be willing to part ways with any routines or behaviours that are further entrenching you in the rut you're trying to escape. Your time audit is a mirror you've held up to your own life, the equivalent of the snapshot we provide to corporations; if you don't like what you see, only you have the power to change it, one habit at a time.

That incremental approach is the one my friend Jann Arden, the singer-songwriter, took when she decided to overhaul her life a decade ago. Her dad was ill and her mother was slipping into Alzheimer's; she needed to prepare herself to be a good caregiver, and she wanted to take better care of herself for her own reasons too. She knew that going cold turkey on all her bad habits at once wasn't realistic, so she shook them off one at a time. First to go: eating junk food and drinking alcohol. Once those were eliminated and she felt she was on firm ground, she decided to start exercising every day—she had the energy to do that, finally. Then she ended a ten-year relationship that had run its course.

Each of these changes required awareness of her own behaviour and its consequences; she came to realize that some of her habits had developed to keep her feelings at bay. Part of her reinvention, then, was retraining herself to figure out what she's feeling and then deal with that feeling, rather than tamping it down with a cupcake or a glass of wine. Jann's always been very creative, obviously, but heightened self-awareness seemed to unlock something inside her. Today she looks radiant, feels fantastic and shifts gears constantly, going from music to writing to acting and business, then back again. Changing her habits didn't just make her healthier—it changed her life and the way she feels about herself.

To break bad habits, you have to know yourself really well and keep holding up a magnifying glass to your own behaviour to figure out why you do the things you do. "Because it's what I've always done" just isn't a good reason. Think *kaizen*. Figure out what your habits are and what purpose they serve—and if it's not your core purpose, get ready to break some of them.

Are you wearing a uniform?

I was recently at a corporate event with a group of (mostly) wealthy women, and the strangest thing happened. As I shook hands with them, I had this feeling that I was meeting the same person over and over. She was very fit and polished, with the same shiny hair. Now, I have no issue with the medical and beauty interventions that were clearly creating some of the homogeneity in the room. If injectables make you feel good about yourself, go for it. What threw me was the fact that I couldn't tell one woman from the next.

It made me think about the unofficial uniforms so many people wear to fit into their social and professional circles, sometimes without even realizing that's what they're doing. There's the busy mom uniform: jeans or leggings, T-shirt, comfortable shoes. And in my industry, the hip guy uniform: black jeans, patterned shirt, funky glasses. Lawyers, I've noticed, often have a very specific lawyerly physical presence. I can always tell when I'm standing next to one in an elevator: the tidiness, the slightly aggressive manner, a sense of performance. The other day I walked into a large meeting of lawyers and was startled to see all of them, about forty men and women, seated at tables in their black and grey suits. There they were, row upon row, like eggs in a carton. No one was distinct. Their "selves" were masked by sameness. It was comical how much I stood out in that room, simply because I was wearing red.

To add another dimension to your self-portrait, figure out whether you're wearing a uniform. I'm not just talking about the way you look, but the way you sound and maybe even the way you think—habits and behaviours that keep you stuck in the same place, spinning your wheels, and may also render you invisible to yourself on some level. *I look like every other receptionist in the building, so that must be who I am.* Of course, if you're perfectly put together but completely comfortable in your own skin and living for yourself, then it's not a uniform—or at least it's one that doesn't constrain you and wasn't imposed on you. Issues arise when the uniform has been fabricated for you by the media or social norms or your own tribe, and you're wearing it not because it's a true expression of your identity but because it feels safe (or obligatory—peer pressure doesn't end when you graduate from high school).

There's no point in kidding yourself: if you want to change, you have to ask yourself tough questions and answer them honestly and objectively. Do you toe the party line in your circle—whether that's trashing the boss, or signing your kids up for every activity under the sun, or clubbing every Friday—not because you want to, necessarily, but because it's the price of admission? Do you resemble every other person in your row of cubicles?

If so, the problem isn't that someone else may not be able to pick you out in a crowd; *you* might lose sight of yourself, who you really are and what you really want. This is what happened to a friend of mine who worked at a prestigious ad agency in New York. He spent his first two decades in the business scrambling up the corporate ladder. His goal: to be CEO of the agency by the time he was forty-five. Smart, talented and one of those genuinely nice people who's liked by everyone, he was named chief operating officer at thirty-nine. Then he stalled. A few years passed, and he was passed over; an outsider was brought in as the new CEO. So he downsized his dream: he wanted to be CEO of any ad agency—a branch office in another country would be fine. When just such an opportunity arose, though, he hesitated. He had no connections in that country, which meant he was unlikely to succeed, and if he failed, it would be very difficult, if not impossible, to return to New York.

For the first time, he started thinking hard about why exactly he wanted to be CEO. The answer? "It was the obvious job to aspire to," he says. The aspiration was built into the New York executive uniform: every ambitious person he knew wanted to be the CEO of something. But he'd been so fixated on getting the top job that he'd lost sight of whether he would actually be good at it, and whether it would even make him happy. No and no, he realized. "I wasn't the guy in the room who inspired other people and sold them on an idea. I wasn't actually good at driving new business—I was more the person offering quiet counsel. My strength was turning situations around and helping people work through problems. Those are two very different skill sets," he says.

"One leads you to be a CEO, and the other leads you to be the number two who makes the CEO look smarter."

Once he realized that the uniform he'd been wearing didn't fit, he also realized that the way he'd been measuring success didn't suit him. It clashed with his core purpose, which was to feel he was really contributing to an organization's success. What mattered to him, then, wasn't an impressive title, but having an opportunity to make a difference by doing what he does best: solving problems.

Becoming the CEO of a small branch office wouldn't be in line with his core purpose, he realized. He wouldn't have much influence, because most major decisions are made back at head-quarters, and he wouldn't even be very good at the job. It would be an empty achievement. So he turned down the offer, which was tantamount to burning his uniform, and left the ad agency to reinvent himself at a global company with tens of thousands of employees. "I wound up creating a new kind of job for myself, one focused solely on problem solving. I have a lot of influence because I directly advise the CEO, and it's really satisfying because I'm dealing with much bigger problems and looking for much bigger solutions than I ever would have running a branch office." It's also more lucrative: his salary is much higher than it would have been if he'd taken the CEO job. And the fact that he's engaged and fulfilled? Priceless.

Reinvention almost always requires shedding whatever uniform you've got on, stepping away from the crowd and putting yourself—your authentic self—out there. It doesn't matter what anyone else thinks you should want or thinks you should be. This is your one and only life. What matters is that you make it the best it can be by your own lights, using your own measures of success.

The benefit of discomfort

It can be startling to realize that you've been living out someone else's dream and it's no longer your own. That's what happened to me after eight seasons on *Dragons' Den*. I was beginning to reinvent my company, and that was where my head was at, even when we were taping the show. My body was on set, but I wasn't really present (funny how things come full circle: in the pre-flood years, I'd checked out emotionally at Venture but was very much present in the Den).

I could actually feel my listening skills eroding; sometimes I had to bite my tongue not to interrupt an entrepreneur mid-spiel, and the pitches started blurring together in my mind. In fact, every step of the process that had once been so invigorating, from getting made up to meeting new people from all walks of life, started to feel a little flat. Not bad, exactly, just . . . easy. Too easy. I'd started on the show without a ton of confidence, but eight years later I was probably *over*confident. The work didn't surprise me anymore, nor did I have to work hard to believe in myself. I showed up and got the job done—and being a Dragon had become just that: a job.

At first I thought I must be burned out, physically and emotionally, but my fatigue magically evaporated whenever I was working on Venture's reinvention. The excitement and uncertainty I felt as I struggled to figure out how to rebuild the company highlighted how habitual *Dragons' Den* had become for me. When I was with my team in Calgary, trying to build something new, I felt alive and excited (and, yes, nervous and anxious too). That made it all the more noticeable that those feelings just weren't present when the cameras started rolling in Toronto.

For me, the original purpose of the show, and its value in my life, was to help entrepreneurs realize their dreams in real time. I loved their passion and the way they bared their hearts and souls. When I lost my own sense of passion, though, I wasn't as effective on camera. To compensate, I'd sometimes find myself exaggerating my reactions a little—acting, in other words, rather than being authentic. But I'm no actress. I'm just not very good at hiding my feelings, which had been a plus when I was hugely engaged in the show, and was a distinct minus when that engagement waned. The only good thing about my sense of detachment was that it allowed me to be objective. The problem wasn't the show. The problem was me. I was wearing a uniform.

Recognizing this made it easier to resist the well-meaning advice I received to hang on to the job for dear life. *Most people would kill to be a Dragon. If you give it up, you'll be replaced in a heartbeat.* Sure, I had moments of insecurity en route to my exit. Was I an idiot, leaving a hit TV show? Being a Dragon was a big part of my identity—how would people see me if I wasn't one?

Then I realized that I didn't care what other people thought. I knew who I was. And one thing I knew for sure about myself was that I wouldn't miss being on camera one iota; nothing exacerbates my physical insecurities more effectively. Still, I hesitated, because there was something I would miss, very much: funding early-stage companies and mentoring entrepreneurs. That tied directly into my core purpose.

Since Venture's new agenda was going to be supporting entrepreneurs, I didn't have to check out of that world entirely, but I hadn't yet figured out how to continue helping smaller but really promising early-stage companies after I left the show. I still believed the best way would be to create the complex ecosystem I'd started dreaming of the night I was "homeless"—but I had no time to figure out what that ecosystem could look like, much less how to fund it. Finally, I realized that I'd never have the time to do my homework unless I stepped off the fast track and left the show.

And that was it. I was finally ready to shrug off my Dragon uniform and head in a new direction. In the end, I felt very good about my decision, because it was right for me but also right for the Den. Just like companies, shows need to evolve; new blood might be the best thing for *Dragons' Den*. One way I knew for sure that leaving was the right move was that it made me feel both excited and a little uncomfortable. I'd just raised the stakes for myself: now I had to do something that vindicated my decision to leave the show. I had to prove to myself that it had been worth it. But hey, no pressure!

Actually, as I discovered when reviewing my own history, I do best under pressure. I enjoy uphill climbs, even though I may bitch and moan during the ascent. The most valuable, most purposeful and most thrilling parts of my life have always been streaked with discomfort. Nothing makes you feel as alive, or as uncomfortable, as navigating uncharted waters. You're not sure what will happen next and how you'll be tested. I wanted to feel that way all the time: alive and as though I was doing my best work, not like I was on autopilot.

Outside the comfort zone

Habits and uniforms really are the enemies of inspiration and innovation. Once you start streamlining old routines and shrugging off an outgrown uniform, you might discover that the rut you're in isn't related to overwork or exhaustion at all. It might simply be, as it was for me, that you've grown complacent. You have an excitement deficit.

After you make some room in your calendar for the excitement of the unknown, your world-weariness may miraculously disappear, leaving you feeling energized rather than worn down. I'm not talking about taking up skydiving or swimming with sharks, but about the excitement that comes from stretching in any new direction. For me, this time, it was about giving up the recognition that comes with a steady TV gig to roll up my sleeves and focus on reinventing my company and myself. Earlier in my life, excitement came from spending more time with my kids, time when I was really focused on them and 100 percent present, not running around trying to get dinner on the table while supervising homework and juggling work calls.

Whatever constitutes excitement for you, pay attention to the feeling. It's a reliable signpost to the kinds of habits you need to break and the changes you need to make.

Abandoning habits, rejigging routines, ditching uniforms, embracing the idea of living differently—it's hard. And that's good. Your willingness to be uncomfortable will open all kinds of doors in your life, and walking through them will change you, for the better. Tolerating discomfort also gives you an advantage over those who won't venture outside their comfort zone. If you persist, you'll build your confidence, too. You'll have shown yourself that you're tougher and more resourceful than you knew.

Which leads directly into the next stage of the process: figuring out what you're really good at, and how to harness whatever that is to your purpose, and then heading in a new direction.

Chapter 6

Currency

Once we've reviewed a company's past and have a good handle on where it is today, we need to get a deeper understanding of its strengths and weaknesses, to figure out what differentiates the brand from its competitors. Often this involves conducting surveys or focus groups, where we ask consumers questions like, Is this a brand you trust? What's unique about it? How is it different from brand X or brand Y? And so forth. The questions are pretty broad, but the answers give you a sense of a brand's strong suit (and where it could improve) and what makes it special.

Particularly in a crowded category, a brand has to offer something unique that people can't get anywhere else. Think about coffee. It used to be that coffee was something you made at home in the morning, or maybe, if you were already out and about, you grabbed a cup to go at a doughnut store or a gas station. It didn't really matter which one, because everyone made coffee pretty much the same way, and served it in the same kind of cups, and charged about the same for it.

All that changed in the 1990s, with the rise of coffee houses. Today, there are a lot of places to drink coffee, at all hours of the night and day, and they have clear differences. At a Nespresso boutique, it's all about the beans. You get a smallish cup of premium coffee in a sleek, modern environment, and you pay a premium price for it. McDonald's is a no-fuss experience, without a lot of fancy options, and the emphasis is on efficiency. Tim Hortons has more of a neighbourhood feel, and the promise of a freshly brewed pot of full-bodied coffee all day long. At Starbucks, there's an endless choice of caffeinated beverages, both hot and cold, and it's all about customization and a personalized experience; it's no accident that the barista calls out your name instead of your order number.

Obviously, there's not just one way to sell coffee. But you do have to know what makes you different, then leverage that difference to create an emotional connection so that coffee drinkers choose you instead of one of your competitors, again and again. Sometimes those differentiators have less to do with the actual product being sold than with the strengths and values of the people behind the brand.

For instance, I'm an investor in a chain of boutique cafés called Balzac's, the brainchild of entrepreneur Diana Olsen, who's a design aficionado and an artistic person—interests that may seem, at first, to have nothing whatsoever to do with coffee. But she used them to differentiate her brand. Inspired by the elegant aesthetic of Parisian cafés (and French novelist Honoré de Balzac's obsession with coffee), she decided to make each Balzac's a beautiful place where people would enjoy the ritual of lingering over a cup of coffee. Sustainability and good health are among her core values, so even though organic milk adds significantly to her costs, she won't budge on carrying it in her cafés, the same way she insists on the artful posters and chalkboard menus that contribute to the contemplative, elevated ambience that sets Balzac's apart. By basing her business on her own personal strengths and values, she successfully differentiated it from all the other coffee places on the block.

Sometimes, figuring out what's unique about a company or a brand is pretty straightforward. For instance, Venture's differentiator was a no-brainer: the people. We'd been in business a long time, so the team had deep marketing experience and skill, and my TV career had given us an unusually high profile. Although our workforce had been more than halved by the flood, those who remained were hard-core believers who wanted the company to survive and had a deep desire to prove they could turn it around. They were scrappy, determined, tenacious, and as committed to our reinvention as anyone could possibly be; their passion was a massive asset and differentiator. Over the years, they've had to do something most people who work at marketing firms do not: they've repeatedly adapted to customers' changing needs, rather than adapting to compete with other agencies, because our focus has always been on our customers, not what everyone else is doing. It has been the secret to our longevity.

Most important, given that we had decided to work exclusively with entrepreneurial businesses, the team was unusually well versed in the entrepreneurial mindset, because they'd been dealing with me for twenty-five years. A lot of entrepreneurial types aren't great process people; we tend to go flying down the field pretty fast, and need other people to fill in the details, execute and put a bow on everything. The team had been doing that with me for so long that there was no question in my mind that they'd be able to do it with other people. All of this combined meant that we had strong currency with entrepreneurs who were looking for a marketing agency, and were therefore well positioned to rebrand Venture as the agency for entrepreneurial types.

Currency + core purpose = superpower

Determining my own professional currency was a little trickier, because Venture's precarious situation had really made me question what I'd always believed about myself. The only thing I knew for sure, now that I was no longer a Dragon, was that I wanted to figure out a new way to support the kinds of early-stage entrepreneurs who appear on the show—and I wanted to go bigger. Much bigger. There wasn't much point in leaving the show only to go smaller.

One idea had occurred to me. If I had more money and the right team behind me, I could back a whole lot more early-stage companies that were looking to scale big. There was really only one way to do that: by raising a venture capital (VC) fund. Essentially, you persuade other people to give you money, and then you invest it in companies that are in need of capital to help them grow. The idea is that, with enough capital, those businesses can grow to the point where, within three to six years, investors will get a strong return on their investment.

"Hey, Arlene, you should start a venture capital fund!" were words that, in my fifty-eight years on the planet, had never come out of anyone's mouth. For one thing, there's my gender: only 2 percent of the funds in Canada are led by women. For another, there's my location: the Prairies get only 6 percent of all the venture capital in the country. And, of course, like any first-time manager, I had zero experience raising tens of millions of dollars. I'd never tried to raise a single dollar, if truth be told, except when I was fundraising for one of the charities I support (and then I'd twist your arm until it fell off or you wrote a cheque, whichever came first). But none of that meant I could not, or should not, try to do it. In fact, in some respects I was uniquely qualified.

If reinventing your life strikes you as an impossible dream, consider this: at an age when I was close to qualifying for a senior's rate at the movie theatre, I decided to try to do something that would be difficult for anyone and was brand new for me—all while trying to save my failing business. Crazy, right? Well, that was what people said in the nineties too, when I was trying to consolidate Western agencies, and I made the mistake of listening to them, which really *was* crazy. The beauty of closing in on sixty is that you've learned a thing or two about naysayers. If they're right and what you're trying to do won't fly, you'll find out soon enough. In the meantime, there's no harm in doing your homework and figuring out whether you have the right stuff to pull off whatever "crazy" thing you've dreamed up.

So did I have the right stuff to raise a fund? I needed to evaluate my currency, by which I don't mean cash but rather what I had in the way of skills that the market would value. Currency is what *you*, and only you, have to offer. It's the sum of all your parts: who you are—your talents, your personality, your values, your experience—and everything you bring to the table, whether that's a huge professional network or a unique ability to understand the zeitgeist. You maximize the value of your currency when you really understand your strengths and assets, and can figure out how to leverage them in this particular time and place.

Lousy as I was feeling about myself in 2014, even I had to admit I had a few things to offer that were unique and valuable. I'd been on TV for a long time—that had to be worth something if I tried to raise a VC fund. At least there was some chance that potential investors might have heard of me, and would be willing to take a meeting.

Another strength: on *Dragons' Den* I'd dealt with countless founders of new companies, so I really did understand how entrepreneurs thought, what they needed, and why some were successful while others were not. I'd backed and supported some of the most successful companies ever to appear on the show, so I certainly did understand how to deploy capital and maximize investments. That was important, because I, not the fund's investors, would select which businesses to back; investors had to have confidence in my ability to pick winners.

In a similar vein, I understood how and why marketing is key to the creation of consumer brands. That expertise was one of my strongest calling cards, in my opinion, because marketing is so important to growth. When you have marketing input at a company's inception, rather than after a product or service has already been created, you can direct growth much more effectively and build something you're sure people will want. I'd already observed that with the companies I'd funded through *Dragons' Den*.

I also had so-called "soft skills" that would be relevant to raising a fund. I'm good at persuading people to do things by showing them how it's in their own best interest—I'd even written a book about it. And to raise millions of dollars, I'd need to do a lot of persuading.

One more thing I had: insight. Learning how to navigate around emotional land mines when I was a little kid made me a good observer. Growing up in a home with a lot of yelling and drama isn't ideal, but in my case it definitely honed my ability to recognize and decode patterns of behaviour. As a child, I never wanted to wade into the fray, where the anger was, so I stayed on the sidelines, alert to every possible threat. Early on, I learned to distinguish between the words and the emotional subtext, how to hear not just what people were saying but what was *really* happening between them. Being a good listener and attending to nuances had given me a lot of insight into people's motivations and behaviour.

When I was first starting out in business, though, it never even occurred to me to think of insight as a marketable skill. How would you frame it on a resumé—"Excellent insight, perfected in dysfunctional family situation"? It wasn't anything I thought could be monetized or parlayed into a career, but it has turned out to be a key differentiator. Listening closely to clients (and to my team at Venture) in order to figure out what really matters to them is the closest thing I have to a superpower. Having insight into people's behaviour also helps me tune in to cultural trends before they fully surface, which is extremely helpful in marketing. It served me well on TV too, where I could pick up on the subtleties in people's pitches that someone else might miss. More generally, listening helps me learn and connect with other people. Virgin co-founder Richard Branson summed it up well when he advised, "Listen more than you talk. Nobody learned anything by hearing themselves speak." To raise a fund, I'd have to do a whole lot of listening and learning.

The concept of currency is helpful because it forces you to think beyond your credentials and work experience and all the other things you'd typically include on your CV, and zero in on the qualities and abilities that differentiate you and are valuable. The trick is to figure out how to amplify them to serve your core purpose, in which case they become superpowers that can help you pull off a reinvention.

Diana Olsen's currency included being highly artistic, which became a superpower when she harnessed it to create a brand of coffee house that was different from anything else out there. For my friend at the New York ad agency, whom I mentioned in the last chapter, his "soft" skill was being good at quietly solving problems, which he leveraged to land a position at a multinational where he whispers advice in the CEO's ear. For me, it was having insight, which I'd need a ton of in order to raise a fund. Insight into the market, insight into the minds of investors, and insight into the abilities and potential of the entrepreneurs whose companies I'd evaluate—I'd need to have all of that in order to persuade anyone to give me a dime.

I'm sure there are lots of people out there who have more impressive qualifications for raising a VC fund, but that didn't mean they'd be better suited to run the kind of fund I envisioned. I did have currency that would be very useful in the food and health sector, and figuring out what it was made me a lot more confident that this was something I should at least try to do.

Everyone has currency

You might be thinking, *I have no currency!* But you do. Everyone does. Nevertheless, many people who want to change their lives get stuck at this stage, because they can't figure out what their currency is, or don't believe it's worth much. For whatever reason, I seem to meet a lot of people who undersell themselves in this way, but one in particular sticks out in my mind: a young soldier I met in Afghanistan.

Over the years, I've spent a fair bit of time visiting Canadian Forces personnel stationed overseas, as part of a program whereby prominent Canadians—actors, musicians, athletes, and even the occasional Dragon—visit the troops. The idea is to thank them for their service, give them a bit of a break, and remind them of the love, respect and gratitude everyone back home has for them. For me, these trips were, hands down, the biggest perk of being on TV, because they are unbelievably inspiring. The bravery and professionalism of our troops is unparalleled, and I've learned so much from them about the complexities of geopolitics. One of the proudest moments in my life was becoming an Honorary Captain of the Royal Canadian Navy; I get to wear the full navy dress, stripes and all. Forget what I said earlier about uniforms—this is the one uniform I'm always honoured to wear and never want to take off.

Until I started spending time with military types, I used to think I was a pretty self-disciplined person. Well, I'm a lightweight compared with them. Their sense of purpose and determination to execute on it is unwavering and impressive as hell.

I'll never forget sitting in the back of a truck heading out of Kabul toward a military base, wearing a flak jacket and helmet. This trip didn't include any celebrities; aside from me, there were just six civilians and military brass, and we'd all come to learn more about Canada's training missions in Afghanistan. Sitting in the truck, we were surrounded by young men in full military gear, clutching machine guns, seemingly oblivious of the forty-degree heat and the clouds of dust swirling around the vehicle. We sped past barbed-wire fences, stopping at large cement barriers every few kilometres. Checkpoints. There had been a bombing on this road only a couple of days before. Every few minutes one of the guys would hop out of the truck and walk ahead of the convoy for a bit. I asked why. "If there are any improvised explosive devices out there, he'll take the IED, not the vehicle," one of the soldiers told me matter-of-factly. It's surreal and overwhelming to realize that somebody is putting his life at risk to protect yours—and everyone is a little blasé about it because, hey, it's all in a day's work.

We arrived safely on the base, thank God, where a small group of trainers proceeded to teach young Afghan men how to operate weaponry. In the middle of this endless desert, the Afghan men stood in several giant circles, each consisting of about a hundred men, with a single Canadian Armed Forces soldier and a translator in the centre. Each circle focused on a different skill: how to load an AK-47, use a tank, operate as a unit. The trainers' command of the situation was absolute, their voices ringing out confidently. It was awe-inspiring.

Afterwards, one of the soldiers on the base sought me out. On these trips, I sometimes get pitched as if we're on a special instalment of the *Den*, set in the desert. Other times, people want to talk hockey or politics. But more than anything else, I get some version of the question that this soldier asked me that day: "I'm retiring from the military in six months—what should I do next?" (At first I couldn't figure out why people thought I was any kind of authority on this subject, but of course many of the people who pitch on the show have given up steady jobs to start their own companies, so I guess I know something about major life changes.)

This soldier was rapidly approaching a crossroads, with no idea which way to turn. All he knew was that his life was about to change, radically, and he didn't feel ready. So I asked, "Well, what is it that you love doing?" But for him, as for many soldiers, that was a tough question to answer. They live highly regulated lives, without a whole lot of free agency. The prospect of rejoining a world where all choices will be their own can be overwhelming. They're often discriminated against, too, when they return to Canada; their skills are woefully undervalued, and they experience higher than average rates of unemployment. Standing there in the blazing heat watching this ultra-competent guy struggle to remember what he loved to do was almost unbearably poignant. He was lost. His core purpose had been to serve his country, and he had, admirably. Now what?

He had no idea, because he didn't know what his currency was. "All I've got is military experience." I was too hot and jet-lagged to be coherent, so I hope he reads the words I wish I'd used: To figure out what your currency is, unbundle your skills from your experience. You need to break down what you've done to its smallest components, then figure out what skills are necessary for each component. A soldier, for instance, has to maintain a high level of physical fitness. The skill you need for that is a huge capacity for self-motivation, as well as the ability to persist through discomfort. Soldiers also have to be able to take direction and work well in a team—key skills in many, many jobs. Plus, this particular soldier had deep logistics training, which hardly anyone in the world has. Oh, and wasn't he serving in a particularly dangerous part of the world, where IEDs were just a fact of life? Why yes. Add "calm, courageous, and good in a crisis" to his currency.

Without even really knowing him or anything about his other talents and interests, I could already identify skills and character traits that are important in fields ranging from teaching to law enforcement to business. In order to do this for himself, he'd need to be able to see himself clearly and observe himself objectively. He'd have to be willing to ask himself a question that's so scary, many people never ask it.

Who am I?

If you think this question is narcissistic, or self-indulgent, then you may *really* need to ask it. There's nothing self-indulgent about self-awareness; without it, you can't understand your impact on others. Nor can you possibly be true to yourself if you don't know who you really are.

Whether you can see your future clearly or, like that soldier, really have no idea what to do next, you do need to know who you are in order to change your life. You need to know what you're capable of, which goals you should stretch to try to reach, and what will make you feel challenged, fulfilled and successful.

This is especially true if you're prone to defining yourself through the uniform you wear, the title you hold or your relationship status. I'm safe on the first two counts but definitely guilty of the third. For a very long time, I measured my worth as a human being by whether I had a man in my life or not. If I was single, I felt there was something wrong with me. If I was in a relationship, even a bad one, I'd hang on longer than I should because, hey, at least I wasn't single.

When I married for the second time, then, the sense of relief was profound. I felt whole at last: someone loved me. I wasn't going to screw this up. My gratitude to the universe, and to this man who had vowed to stand by me till death do us part, was immense. When, after a few years of marriage, he told me that his aspiration was to run a company, I gladly offered him mine, and made him president of Venture. I was still CEO, but he was running the day-to-day operations of the company.

Fast-forward past some wonderful moments and some terrible lows, to the seventh year of our marriage. One day we got home from work and my husband told me to sit down. He needed to tell me something. It was evident from his tone that this would not be good news, and he seemed to have rehearsed a speech. He'd clearly been working up to this moment for a long time. There, in the living room of the home we'd been building together, he told me that he didn't love me anymore, and hadn't for years. I shattered. This was the person I was going to spend the rest of my life with. There was a gap between who I'd thought he was and what he was now telling me that made no sense. He looked entirely unfamiliar to me.

As he walked out the door, I felt entirely unfamiliar to myself, too. Who was I, if not this man's wife? I truly had no idea. In the course of an hour, I'd gone from feeling whole to feeling broken, undesirable and unbelievably stupid. I'd spent so long projecting strength, a necessity for a CEO, that I'd neglected my interior life to the point where I didn't really have one anymore. This is one reason my husband's rejection wounded me as deeply as it did. I didn't know myself well enough to have a lot of convictions about myself, so I didn't question his. I took them on as gospel truth, then layered on my own interpretation. If he didn't love me, that meant I was unlovable. If he didn't desire me, I was undesirable. Without his affirmation, I could see no positives. Only negatives.

Of course, there had been signs over the previous few years that things weren't right, but I'd ignored them. I defined myself through my marriage, and therefore didn't want to question it. Besides, my husband was one of those nice guys whom everyone loves; if he wasn't all that nice to me, the problem was clearly mine. I just needed to be sexier, thinner, more mysterious, more exciting, is all. I believed that I could change, and become the woman he wanted me to be.

To do that, I'd have to get better at business, too. After taking a six-week executive course at Harvard, he'd returned to Calgary convinced that Venture needed to be managed differently. I hadn't taken the course—he hadn't even wanted me to attend his graduation, though I'd paid for the course, speaking of warning signs—and he was very persuasive. He spoke with such passion about the need to implement some of the new theories he'd learned that I believed he must be right. He had a university degree, and now this certificate from Harvard, of all places. Of course he knew more than I did! I had experience, but that was all. I was thankful that he was going to step in and correct my mistakes, and encouraged him to make the changes he thought were necessary. In the back of my mind, of course, was another thought: *Maybe now he'll be warm and loving again.*

When, shortly before he announced that he didn't love me, he began urging me to sell the company, it didn't occur to me that he might have anything other than my best interests at heart. Quite possibly he did. I'll never know for sure. The only certainty is that if I'd listened, he would have received half the proceeds from the sale when we divorced and my life would have unfolded very differently than it has. I very much doubt that I would have become a Dragon, or that you'd be holding this book in your hands. Fortunately, I didn't act on his urging, but I did listen to him. And what I heard, though it may not have been what he meant, was, "This business will never be a success with you at the helm."

When he left me, then, I felt unmoored, both personally and professionally. If you'd asked me what my currency was, I wouldn't have been able to answer. Ditto if you'd asked me who *I* was, and what I wanted out of life. All I wanted, at that moment, was for my husband to come back and love me again. I could not see a way to feel better unless he did. The prospect of having to continue seeing him every day in the office was beyond horrible. The humiliation of being rejected, of being unloved, was all tangled up with my work, which had always been a source of solace and pride. I cried my eyes out all weekend, then went into the office on Monday, gathered everyone around, and told them that, regrettably, the president of the company and I were separating, but it was business as usual. People were kind. They said all the right things. And then they went back to work.

So did I, but the next few months were exquisitely awkward and painful. It took every ounce of self-control I had to conduct myself professionally during meetings that included my soon-to-be ex-husband. I was so hurt, upset and embarrassed that I wanted to crawl under a rock, but instead, I tried to act as though I was just fine. Anything else would harm the business. I felt as vulnerable and exposed as a newborn, only no one was taking caring of me. I was the CEO. Taking care of people was *my* job. I was hyper-conscious of how uncomfortable the situation was for everyone around us, especially after we had a loud argument one afternoon in the office, but also overwhelmed by the lack of privacy: our breakup was playing out in daily instalments, in front of an audience. The office had always been a refuge for me, but now it was more like a torture chamber.

The pressure built and built, until it felt unbearable. I'd long prided myself on my ability to power through the hard stuff and bounce back pretty fast. When my kids were young, I couldn't spend too much time licking my wounds—I was a single mom, so I had to take care of them, and model strength and resilience. So I got good at smoothing things over, even my own feelings. But this time was different. I stopped eating, stopped sleeping. My coping skills fell away. I was so pale and drawn that one of my daughters insisted I get a checkup, so I dragged myself to the doctor's office.

I remember waiting for my doctor, legs dangling off the examination table, looking at the posters on the wall. One screamed, ARE YOU SUFFERING FROM DEPRESSION? I read through the list of symptoms. *Loss of interest in previously enjoyable activities. Low energy. Feelings of helplessness.* Check. Check. Check. I had all of the symptoms. When my doctor came in, she asked, "How are you doing?"—and I burst into tears. You know how sometimes your feelings are so raw that if someone shows you just the tiniest shred of sympathy, or says something banal but kind, it triggers all kinds of emotions? I told her exactly how I was feeling, and why.

She suggested antidepressants. I barely remember picking up the prescription, but I do recall standing in the bathroom when I got home, staring at the bottle of little white pills for what felt like forever. There had been a lot of different medications in my house growing up, and I have family members whose lives have been dramatically improved by antidepressants. But I was afraid to take them. Honestly, I was afraid I'd never be able to stop taking them. So I put the bottle of pills in a drawer and closed it.

In a way, they'd already done their job, by forcing me to confront a fact I'd been denying: *this is serious*. It is serious when you don't know who you are. It is serious when you take your measure externally, by what someone else thinks of you. It is serious when you feel worthless.

But as Eleanor Roosevelt said, "No one can make you feel inferior without your consent." I needed to withdraw my consent, and reclaim my life. The only good thing to say about the scorched earth my marital split left behind was that it had cleared a space for me to do that.

Am I worth it?

I'd never actually spent meaningful time on my own—on purpose, I mean, and because I wanted to. While I was launching a business and raising a family, it was impossible. But here I was on the eve of my fifty-first birthday, single again and as lost as that soldier I'd later meet in Afghanistan. Spontaneously, I decided to take a trip. Alone. I had never taken a holiday on my own before. I'd been in plenty of hotel rooms on business trips, sure, but travelling for pleasure had always seemed like something I'd do later, or with someone else. Well, there was no one else anymore. I suddenly wondered: is later now?

For years, I'd dreamed of going to Thailand, but I'd always told myself that the timing wasn't right, it would take too long to get there, I couldn't possibly leave Venture for a few weeks—I had a lot of good excuses. The bottom line, though, was that I just didn't feel I deserved a big trip. I have no problem writing a big cheque for a charity or plunking down a hefty amount to help another entrepreneur get to the finish line faster. But it felt weirdly shameful and self-indulgent to think of being as generous to myself. I felt I simply wasn't worth it.

I'm sure that just about everyone has experienced this low-worth feeling at some point, but for women it's especially familiar. We internalize a whole vocabulary of denial and sacrifice that men don't have to deal with, messages like: *I should be happy with what I have. Taking care of myself is self-indulgent. My real responsibilities are to other people.* Whenever I'm at a large, family-style dinner, I always notice that women take the worst cut of meat from the platter. We all saw our mothers do that, right? It is so deeply ingrained in me that still, even today, I take the worst piece!

When I started looking at the cost of flights to Thailand, I almost called the whole thing off. It was a lot of money. Few men who run companies would feel they had to justify an expensive trip—they'd just assume they'd earned it, damn it, and so would everyone around them—but I sure did. Then the universe handed me an excellent reason to fly halfway around the globe. I learned that my ex, who was no longer at Venture, was in a serious relationship with a woman who'd also recently left the company. That was it. I wasn't going to sit around humming along to "How Long Has This Been Going On?" and driving myself crazy. I fired off an e-mail to an ex–Venture staffer who'd started a travel company based in Bangkok (speaking of reinventions!) and asked him to plan an itinerary for me.

I'd never done anything like this in my life, and getting on the plane felt surreal, dangerous, exciting and extravagant, all at once.

But as soon as I fastened my seat belt, my courage went *poof*. I remember thinking, *Oh my God, I've got to get off. What am I doing, going to the other side of the world at my age? Alone?!* I was seriously considering deplaning when a man settled into the seat next to mine and said hello. I've always thought of myself as an introvert, not someone who strikes up conversations with strangers, but I didn't want to be rude. So I said hello back, and we began to talk. A pleasant middle-aged guy, my seatmate told me his ultimate destination wasn't Thailand but Nepal. He'd been there several times already, mountain climbing, and he described the freedom of the ascent and the beauty of Mount Everest with such passion that I barely noticed our flight taking off.

I've always believed in "accidental mentors"—those people you meet, seemingly at random, who change the way you see things. This man was one of those. He told me that on his last trip one of the Sherpas guiding his group had died on the mountain. This guy had raised funds for the Sherpa's widow and children once he returned to Canada, and was now flying to Nepal with a large cheque to make sure the kids could continue their education and the family didn't fall into poverty. While there, he'd participate in a memorial ceremony for the lost Sherpa at the base of the mountain. The future of this family weighed heavily on him, it was clear. Then he asked me where I was going, and why.

"Well, I'm going to Thailand. To find myself, I guess," I said, feeling more than a little sheepish. My own trip sounded so frivolous by comparison.

"That's very courageous," said the man, and he sounded sincere. I felt like, *Okay, if this guy who has scaled mountains and has the integrity to fly across the world to take responsibility for another man's family is telling me I'm courageous, I'll take it.* Already, the way I saw myself was shifting.

I never saw him again, but I carried that guy's affirmation of my courage with me like a precious jewel as I made my way around Thailand. I meditated for the first time in my life in the mountains, visited the tallest building in Bangkok, cycled back roads in Chiangmai. I met kind-hearted people everywhere I went, people who were eager to try out their English or tell me something about their country or ask about mine. I realized with a start that the label of "introvert" was something that had been imposed on me, and wasn't entirely accurate. Maybe it never had been. Turned out I *enjoyed* meeting strangers and finding out about their lives. I even started to enjoy eating alone in restaurants, and striking up conversations with the wait staff and other diners.

After my marriage ended, I'd been so consumed with shame and concern about what others might be thinking or saying about me, but now I was focused outward, on what I was experiencing. Of all the incredible moments on that trip, I most remember kayaking down the Mekong River, the thick jungle pressing in on both sides. The birds made the most amazing, symphonic sounds. The sun was hot, but I felt strong and alert to the world. I recognized courage in myself, as well as confidence in my own competence, for the first time in years.

Alone, on the other side of the world, I was very far out of my comfort zone, and that forced me to view myself in a new light. I didn't have my professional identity or my mom identity to fall back on; they meant nothing when I was trying to keep my kayak from tipping. I didn't have a man to lean on, or carry the luggage, or eat dinner with. Every moment was up to me. At first that felt strange and a little frightening, until I realized something: it had always been true. My life had always been up to me.

I had to choose what to make of it. I could feel categorically unlovable, or I could conclude that my husband didn't love me and therefore I was better off on my own. I could feel worthless, or I could recognize that I was worth it, whether the question was "Should I take a holiday?" or "Should I try to do something difficult?"

When a relationship ends, it can leave you feeling lessened, but it also leaves you with lessons. Here's the most important one I took away: when I let my relationships define me, it's a cop-out, really, a way of abdicating responsibility for the kind of person I am and what I make of myself. It's like handing someone else the keys to my life and saying, "Here, you drive."

Even someone who loves you, honours you and would never intentionally cause you harm can't steer your course as well as you can. They don't know what's inside you, your deepest fears, yearnings, talents and aspirations. Only you can know all that—and if you don't already, then it's time to figure it out. Who you are, and what matters to you, is the basis of your currency.

Detective work

Everything that's going to power your reinvention is inside you, so you need to know what you've got. Taking inventory is simple, but not easy. Start by logging your strengths. Literally. Write them down on a piece of paper or a computer, in whatever order they come to you. Intellectual, emotional, social, professional—you're aiming to catalogue everything you've got.

Stuck already? Good news: in marketing, we use a range of different techniques to tease out brands' strengths, and most can easily be adapted for your purposes. Bear with me, because I'm going to be unleashing a bunch of different strategies here, and you may be tempted to plow right through the next few pages. But I strongly encourage you to put the book down and try to complete each exercise. I'm hoping that one will be a game changer that will help you evaluate what you have to offer in a whole new way.

Start by going back to your time audit. Which hours left you feeling the most fulfilled? Let's say the answer is "going on the school field trip with my son." Here's your follow-up question: why? What exactly did you enjoy—being with your child while he discovered something new, or the educational aspect of the trip, or interacting with a large group of kids, or bonding with the teacher, or simply getting out of the house or away from your desk and moving around? When you really drill down to the "why" of your most enjoyable, fulfilling times, almost always you'll hit a vein of competency (most of us don't enjoy or feel fulfilled by activities and experiences that make us feel incompetent). You may discover a piece of currency such as "I'm good with kids, they listen to me and like me," or "I can stay alert and focused even in the midst of mayhem," or "I'm good at making a boring museum exhibit come alive." Whatever the answer, add it to your list: it's currency.

A second technique marketers use in focus groups to determine a brand's currency is to ask people, "If this brand were a person and walked into the room right now, what would he or she be like?" It's astonishing how detailed a personality portrait people will draw of a bottle of baby shampoo ("She's gentle and quiet-spoken, but stands up for herself") or a minivan ("He's jolly and outgoing, not all that bright"). Try turning this around, so that *you're* the brand. What would people in a focus group say about you? What would they find interesting or intriguing? How might they describe you? What might they think your currency is? Even if you're the kind of person who bats away compliments, insisting you don't deserve them, record your answers. Ditto if you're the type who tosses and turns at night, fretting about what people think of you. Remember, the goal here isn't to torture yourself but to induce some objectivity and imagine the first impression you make on others.

If you're still coming up empty-handed, and are convinced that your currency is either non-existent or has no value, ask yourself these sorts of questions: What would have happened in my last job if I hadn't been there? What would have happened last night at home if I hadn't been there? What wouldn't have got done? What disaster might have occurred? Who would still be pissed off if I hadn't intervened and done x, y, z? The "if I hadn't been there" exercise can be applied to just about any setting, ranging from the sports team you played on in high school to your book club. Your presence does make a difference in some way (admittedly, occasionally that difference is negative). Something wouldn't have happened, or wouldn't have worked, or wouldn't have worked as well, if you hadn't been there. Whatever that "something" is speaks directly to your currency and what you're good at, so make a note of it.

The reason this exercise is powerful is that it forces you to consider the contribution you make from a different perspective. For instance, if you're in a field where sales really matter but you're only so-so at sales, your absence might not have a dramatic impact on sales, and you might beat yourself up about that. But if you're the person who calms down angry clients, or persuades the volatile genius in the office not to quit, or comes up with ways to cut costs without firing anyone, your absence would most definitely have a huge impact on the bottom line. When you assess what you bring to the table not only in the "outright wins" category but also in the "crises and losses averted" category, you begin to understand the difference you're making. Drum roll, please: your currency.

Another approach we take in marketing is to interview outsiders, which is also a good way to get a handle on your strengths. But since you're not in the market for empty compliments, you need to ask really targeted questions, just as we do in focus groups. If you lob a softball like "Do you think I'm good at anything?" most people will blow smoke. Once you ask a very direct question that touches right on someone else's own area of expertise, however, the conversation gets a whole lot more real. "You're in finance—do you think it's a field where my skills would be valued? Why or why not?" Or, "My degree is in Russian literature—could that help me if I wanted to go into your field and become a realtor?" Or, "I want to get into retail, but you're the expert—is there anything about my background that would help me do that?"

The key to good interviewing is really listening and asking follow-up questions, not frantically planning what you're going to say next. Make it clear that you're not applying for a job (not just yet, anyway) but rather are trying to get different perspectives on your skill set, and what you're looking for is honest, unvarnished feedback. This is a fact-finding mission, and you want every scrap of information you can get, so don't be put off if someone says, "Hell no, your background is all wrong for this industry." Find out *why* it's all wrong, and what that person's perception is of your background. Sometimes you discover, as I suspect the soldier I met in Afghanistan has, that you've done a less than stellar job of explaining who you are and what you've done, so the other party truly has no idea what your skills and talents actually are.

If, like me, you already have an idea of how you want to reinvent, you should know after completing these exercises whether you've got the currency to try to pull it off, or whether you need to upskill or go back to the drawing board altogether. If, however, you started with no real sense of what your new direction should be, look at the list of strengths you've just compiled. See if any pattern lifts off the page. That shape you're seeing? It's the outline of your reinvention.

Currency = confidence

I've spent many years corralling, cutting, colouring, experimenting with and despairing about my head of curls. Against all odds and to my great amusement, my hair has become something of a personal trademark. The times when I've coloured over my streak, people have come up to me on the street, agitated, demanding an explanation. I need a hairdresser who gets all that, and I have one: Beverly Robertson.

Because I travel so much, I sometimes ask her to come to my home at six in the morning to do my hair. I feel bad asking anyone to do anything at that hour, but she is the consummate professional. She never says no and she never acts as though it's an imposition. She always shows up exactly when she says she will, and no matter the crazy hour, she radiates positive energy. Those pre-dawn sessions are more intimate than a salon visit, because it's just us and our cups of coffee, and I've come to know Beverly very well as a person, not just as the person who tames my hair. She'd been with her salon for fifteen years and, sure, had dreamed of starting her own place, but it seemed so risky and she really had no idea where to start. I knew she had dedication, talent and an incredible work ethic—strong currency for a successful reinvention. But Beverly really didn't know her own value, so she lacked the confidence to try to rewrite her own story.

On a whim one day, I suggested that she come with me to Toronto to do my hair for a special episode of *Dragons' Den*. She was nervous. *What if I'm not good enough? I mean, the people who work on TV are the best of the best. I'm just a hairdresser from Calgary.* Nevertheless, she got on the plane and, of course, everyone on set loved her. She was a star. With every compliment, I swear I could see her confidence blooming. I was watching a reinvention in real time.

When she got back to Calgary, Beverly walked into the salon where she was employed and suddenly her self-doubt was gone. "It was like a light switch had been hit," she later told me. She realized that she couldn't spend one more second working for somebody else. "It was the feeling of a bride running away from the altar. It was so deep." That was a Monday. On Tuesday, she quit.

What might have looked impulsive was actually the result of fifteen years of preparation. All that time, Beverly had been building her currency, but only when she ventured outside her comfort zone did she realize that she already had more than enough to buy herself a new kind of life. "I learned there was a world outside my little world—a little world that I had thought was the only possibility for me," she said.

Suddenly, as often happens in a reinvention, everything else in her life started changing too. She had been engaged, and she called off the wedding. I felt for her—that is not an easy decision—but I wasn't surprised. I've seen similar scenarios over and over: the rising confidence necessary to change your life goes hand in hand with the confidence to reinvent, or leave, relationships that simply no longer make you happy. She also cut ties with the toxic people in her life who responded to her desire to make more of herself with sneers rather than cheers.

While all this was going on, she was busy researching the business potential of a salon that would reinvent the experience of getting your hair done. Her plan was to design a place that reflected her personality—her superpower in a line of work that's all about connecting with and understanding other people. Beverly is that rarest of combinations: her personal style is hip and chic, but she is incredibly warm and friendly. She wanted her salon to be like that too: a luxurious, beautiful, attitude-free zone, not one of those fancy places with snooty staff who make you feel you're not cool enough to be there. She wanted the experience to be welcoming, not intimidating—just like her. So she decided to eliminate the front desk altogether and change the relationship between the customer and the stylist: the client would pay the stylist directly, she decided, via iPad. She imagined a space with wine and cookies and a business bar where people could plug in their laptops and get a bit of work done while they were getting their hair cut and coloured. It would be like hanging at your most stylish girlfriend's house, free of judgment and all about comfort.

As a talented, in-demand stylist with a loyal following, Beverly's network was another key aspect of her currency. She turned to family and friends for advice and even a literal helping hand, like ripping out the walls in her newly rented salon. I was flattered when she asked me for input (and delighted that she didn't ask me to help put up new drywall), and I'll bet others were too. But here's the thing: she did have to ask. Her network wouldn't have been worth much in the early stage of her new business if she hadn't had the confidence to reach out and ask for help. People you already know are like levers: they can't help lift you up unless you activate them.

Beverly's drive, talent, personality and network are the core of her currency, but its value is greatly increased by her understanding of the cultural moment. She knew that clients wanted a sleek, modern-looking salon that was also comfortable and homey. She knew they wanted a more relaxed salon experience, where the vibe is upbeat and friendly, not intimidating. And she knew that customers wanted a place where they could multi-task and keep working, and get in and out quickly rather than waiting at reception both to check in and to pay. Her understanding of market trends—an understanding she's been forging for years—is a major advantage.

That said, it was a tough transition. While getting the physical space ready, she had to live off her dwindling savings and put in fifteen-hour days. But instead of feeling exhausted, she was energized by the challenges. "My fear of failing was less than my desire to win," she said. "I knew that I would die trying to make it happen, and if I didn't try, I would regret it." Focusing on preventing regret helped slay the fear and any vestiges of self-doubt.

Beverly has all the pieces in place for a successful reinvention. She changed her story from "It's too scary" to "It's too scary not to." And she had the confidence, finally, to declare who she is through her business. It's all about *her* vision and *her* purpose and *her* strengths, which is why I know she's going to succeed. Currency is about using everything at your disposal to make your unique mark, the way Beverly is. She probably won't make head-lines (though trust me, her blow-outs are worthy of them), but she is already making a whole new life for herself.

The name of her salon? Appropriately enough, it's The Beverly.

Understanding your currency makes you adaptable

Understanding your currency won't just help you propel yourself to success, it will also carry you through the lean times. After three decades in the music business, Jann Arden knows a thing or two about that. Some songs just don't land and some albums just don't sell, no matter how beautiful the melodies and clever the lyrics.

"You're not always going to be on top," she says. "I feel bad for anyone who thinks it's going to be up, up, up. It won't be, so you better know who you are, and be comfortable with that. I long ago stopped trying to make music that catered to the radio. I don't give a shit about any of those measures of popularity. As far as criticism or social media or people telling me, 'You can't do that!' or 'You should look like that!'—please. It doesn't even get past my hairline. I don't pay any attention."

She's in a business where singers go in and out of style like flared jeans, and yet she's still thriving. Why? Because she understands her currency—humour, no-BS authenticity, artistry and a way with words—well enough to leverage it in many different ways. A master reinventor, Jann is also a published poet, author, TV host, documentary producer and animal rights activist. And, oh yeah, we do a podcast together too. Tastes and habits change, but she's able to adapt and change direction—not because she's a chame-leon, but because the opposite is true. Her main selling point is simply that she is never less than completely herself, regardless of the venue, the audience or the medium.

Knowing your currency makes you adaptable, and in Jann's view that's the secret to a good life. "Human beings weren't meant to have a job for fifty years, to put in the time and get the pension. We're not meant to be placid," she says. "The fact is, you're going to drop dead. You might die in a week, you might die in fifty years. So get out there more and try different things. I don't care if you're seventy-five years old. Every single day you have a choice to make—'How big am I going to live?'"

If you do decide to go big, you need to understand not only your currency but your context: what's valued in this particular place and time. Fortunately, that's something marketers understand better than just about anyone. Read on, and I'll show you how we do it.

Chapter 7

Context

Once we really understand a company's currency, we're ready to define and position its brand. First, though, we have to test whether our concept will fly, by gauging the market. How big is it, and how quickly is it growing? What do consumers want, and what turns them off? Which companies are dominant in the space? Understanding what you're up against is crucial if you want to succeed.

To assess the market thoroughly, we conduct our own small focus groups, access the seemingly never-ending supply of market data generated by research firms, and tap into digital social listening tools to "see" what people are talking about and care about on social media channels. One thing we're looking at is demographics: who buys this type of product, and why. If you've ever completed an online survey after visiting a retail site, or agreed to participate in a phone survey, you know the kinds of questions marketers ask: What problem does this product solve for you? Would you recommend this brand to a friend? We're trying to figure out why you buy stuff, and what you think of our client's product versus all the other ones out there. We're looking for opportunities and unmet needs in the market.

Let's say you're a manufacturer of paper towels and your sales have flatlined, so you hire a marketing firm to help drive growth. It's not an exciting, sexy product, but it's one that we all use just about every day, which is good news and bad news. Good news: there's pretty steady demand for paper towels. Bad news: the market is mature and not growing all that much from one year to the next. Plus, there are already quite a few well-established brands, so getting a better toehold will be difficult.

One obvious way to do it would be to undercut everyone else on price, but that would likely mean you couldn't afford to do much in the way of marketing, and would therefore have difficulty rebuilding your brand. If you ever tried to raise the price again, you'd probably lose any customers you'd gained; they wouldn't have any loyalty to the brand, because all it would stand for is "cheap." Once that was gone, they would be too.

Another way to turn things around would be to innovate: invent a truly disruptive product with the potential to change the whole market. Let's say you came up with a paper towel that could be used ten times instead of just once. That would make our job as marketers easy. We could position your brand as being environmentally friendly as well as cost-effective, because people wouldn't need to buy paper towels as frequently. The market potential could be huge, if—and it's a very big if—you could manufacture these magical paper towels in a cost-efficient manner, and charge consumers about the same as your competitors do. You'd also need to be poised to adapt once your competitors ripped off your technology and introduced their own reusable paper towels.

In order to win in an established, slow-growing market, you have to identify an unmet need—whether that's the need for a really cheap version of the product, or an indestructible one, or whatever—and then meet it, to try to get more traction. Let's say that our research indicated that people are willing to pay more for paper products when the manufacturers have really great sustainability programs; we'd advise you to implement one, and then we could build a marketing campaign around it. Or maybe research showed that consumers would really like paper towels designed to match their decor; we'd suggest that as an avenue for your company, and we'd knock ourselves out trying to come up with a cool ad campaign to publicize it.

Research, however, is just a guide, not a god. Markets can be disrupted without a whole lot of warning, and then all your great research may go right out the window. Think about electric cars, and how quickly they disrupted the automobile industry, essentially creating a whole new class of vehicle—one that's exciting, intriguing and environmentally conscious, so it's basically God's gift to marketers. It doesn't get much better than that. If you have a great idea and can educate people on why they should change their habits and embrace this new thing, whether it's electric cars or ride sharing, you can upend an existing market or create a brand new one. (See why I wanted Venture to focus on entrepreneurial businesses that are all about disrupting mature markets?)

This is one reason we don't just investigate the market for our client's product but also consider broader cultural changes. We look at what's going on in the world generally, to try to anticipate market shifts. If the keto diet is all the rage, that could have a negative impact on the market for products that are high in carbs but a positive impact on, say, swimsuit sales. If fear of terrorism is on the rise, that might hurt airlines but help local tourist attractions. Knowing what's going on in the world is really important, so that you can make trends work for you, not against you.

The bottom line is that we need a clear understanding of context—what's important and valuable in this particular place and time—in order to pinpoint market opportunities and potential pitfalls, and maximize the value of our clients' currency. Understanding context is also important for maximizing the value of your personal currency. As with the loonie, the value of your currency fluctuates depending on external factors. The better you understand the market, the better you'll be at spotting opportunities and seizing them.

Exchange rates fluctuate

I've met some incredibly successful people whose ideas seem to explode out of the gates with impeccable timing, right when the world is looking for just what they are offering. There may be some luck involved, but their success usually has more to do with their understanding of cultural context. Here's the really interesting part: they're dialed in to the world, yes, but they're dialed in to themselves first. They *really* understand their own currency. Their self-awareness seems to give them a sort of X-ray vision that enables them to spot a cultural moment or opportunity that jibes with their own passions and needs, then power forward to capitalize on it, with uncanny accuracy.

When I first started on *Dragons' Den*, I became friends with a producer named Lisa Gabriele, who's really, really good at what I've just described. Because she understands her currency so well, she knows that there are many different ways she could use it. Lisa is perceptive, funny and very reassuring, so she was adept at calming my newbie nerves, but she could also use those three traits to reinvent herself as a therapist or teacher if she were so inclined.

An even more unusual skill she has is being able to create a coherent pattern out of a jumble of scraps, which is vital for editing but also many other kinds of work, ranging from forensics to diagnostic medicine to public policy formation. And very unusually for the world of reality TV, where sensationalism and on-camera blunders and conflict are ratings gold, she has a strong moral compass. I came to trust that she would cut episodes in a way that made me look like a competent, savvy Dragon; a bad edit can change the meaning of a scene completely and make you look like someone you're not, but I always felt safe in her hands. That strong sense of right and wrong, along with the ability to see patterns, would have made her a pretty awesome attorney. If I were ever accused of a crime I didn't commit, I'd definitely want a lawyer with those skills.

When I first met her, Lisa was only in her early forties but had already held a dizzying variety of jobs: journalist, radio writer, ghostwriter, showrunner, TV writer and producer. If she were to do a self-audit, the common thread in all those pursuits would be storytelling. The form of her storytelling changes from job to job, but it is her superpower, and always the foundation of each new incarnation. So I was not surprised, though I was heartbroken, when she decided to leave the show in 2012. She wanted to write a novel. A lot of people want to write novels, but it's hard to write a good one and also hard to get a publisher to buy it. Publishing is a pretty high-risk business, so there's a preference for authors such as James Patterson, J.K. Rowling and Stephen King, whose brands are already well-established and whose fans can be relied on to buy whatever they write.

In 2012, however, *Fifty Shades of Grey* was all the rage, and Lisa had had a brainstorm: she could write an edgier erotic novel, one with a decidedly feminist bent. She could break into fiction writing by capitalizing on a cultural moment. She pitched a sex-positive romance trilogy called *S.E.C.R.E.T.* to publishers and, in a fierce bidding war, sold the rights around the world. Later, she had the ultimate gratification of seeing her pen name—L. Marie Adeline—on bestseller lists for months.

Of course, she didn't know all this would happen when she quit the show. No question, it would have been easier for her to say, "I'd love to write a novel, but all I've ever done is write the truth, so . . . Someday." Or, "Publishing is so different from television—I'd better spend a year or two getting up to speed on this new industry." Or, "If I leave TV, I might fail, and then where would I be?"

Her decision to leave the show called for courage, but mostly it required an understanding of a cultural trend and rock-solid faith in her own currency. Otherwise, she wouldn't have had the confidence to bet on her own ability to reinvent herself. But she was confident, because she figured that a storyteller in one medium has a better than average chance of succeeding in another, and she also recognized that she had a golden opportunity to take advantage of a trend. She knew, too, that the opportunity was time-limited, so she had to act quickly. Her ability to write an erotic novel hadn't been worth very much pre–*Fifty Shades*, and when the trend waned, the value of her currency would plummet again. So she needed to strike at the top of the market, when every publisher in the world was scrambling to find the next blockbuster erotic romance novel. Sure enough, the craze did pass after a few years, but true to form, Lisa had already moved on and written another bestselling novel, this time under her own name in a completely different genre: suspense. I have no doubt she'll be doing something different again a few years from now. Whatever it is, I'm sure she'll make a success of it, because she really understands how to adapt her currency when the context changes.

When you're clear on both your currency and the context, you can bust genres and boundaries the way Lisa Gabriele has, over and over again. Awareness of the ways the world is changing helps you know when you need to change too. And self-awareness enables you to jump on opportunities the way she did, instead of wringing your hands, wondering whether you've got what it takes, and missing the boat altogether. When you understand both how to use who you are and how to read what's going on around you, you can stay a step ahead of the times.

Timing matters

Sometimes currency and context don't line up quite so neatly, though, and the result is either a near miss or a near hit, depending on how you see the world. I've had a couple of those myself. Years ago, in the early days of the Internet, I was sitting on a plane looking at my pager—one of those bygone devices that you only see now in movies about drug dealers set in the nineties. At the time, however, my pager was cutting edge and had just been connected to e-mail. I remember sitting on the plane, looking at my e-mails floating across the tiny pager screen, thinking how bizarrely magical it was, and then suddenly wondering, *Is this actually private?* If my messages were pinging around in the ether, I reasoned, maybe someone else could see them too. As a marketer, I knew all too well how valuable personal information is—it's the basis of our research. At the time, Mark Zuckerberg was probably in diapers.

I distinctly remember having an insight on that plane: *One day the whole world is going to be trying to collect our information. And eventually people are going to say, "No, I don't want to give up my personal data for free."*

When I got home, I immediately bought the URL guardmyprivacy.com. I had an idea that it might be possible to disrupt the whole media environment as well as the marketing industry. I could start a business protecting people's personal information, so that companies would have to pay consumers to get it, bypassing media companies altogether. If an advertiser wanted to target me for a particular type of ad, they'd have to pay me directly for the privilege. Admittedly, I didn't have all the kinks worked out, but the premise was sound: give consumers control over their personal information and a way to monetize it.

And then . . . nothing came of it. I wasn't ready, but neither was the world. Back then, Internet commerce was in its infancy and you could read just about any newspaper online for free; the idea of paying to protect your privacy, of all things, was a very hard sell. Most people didn't even know that their personal data was being collected when they went onto a website. Being online felt anonymous: you could look at anything you wanted, say anything you wanted in a chat room, and no one would ever know it was you! The idea that Google was tracking every mouse click, and could turn around and sell your personal data to advertisers, hadn't crossed many people's minds yet. The concept of user privacy simply didn't have traction, because most people mistakenly thought their privacy was already being protected.

I met with a few people in the tech sector who knew better, but I didn't have the right currency to champion the cause. I'm not a tech person, and I'm not fully fluent in their language. Nor did I really rally my resources and pull all the levers I might have. Eventually, I moved on to the next idea and mostly forgot about this one. But it came to mind in a neon flash when Mark Zuckerberg was testifying before Congress, apologizing for the massive privacy breaches that Facebook permitted during the 2016 presidential election. So much for guarding our personal data.

My timing was off. I had misread the context and arrived too soon, carrying the wrong currency. (If somebody reading this wants to run with the idea, go for it.) But I don't chalk it up as a loss. Here's the thing: if you're tuned in to yourself and the world, you're going to have a lot of ideas for reinvention. Some will hit, some will miss. If your idea doesn't connect with the culture, you need to keep looking—and listening, observing, learning and asking questions. If you do, you will eventually find an idea that does connect.

I've had a thousand ideas since guardmyprivacy.com, some of them really good and some of them . . . not. The ones that have struck gold are the ones that I believed in passionately, and where I had both the correct currency *and* an accurate read on the cultural context.

Intelligence gathering

In 2014, as we were struggling to rebuild and rebrand Venture, I was pretty sure I had one of those golden ideas. It hadn't come to me in a eureka! flash, the way guardmyprivacy.com had. It was more of a slow build, courtesy of the reinvention process I've been describing throughout this book.

The idea: to raise a VC fund and build an ecosystem for entrepreneurs in the food/beverage and health sectors. There was nothing like it in Canada, and if it worked, it would be a game changer. It would also make an entrepreneur out of me, because it had disruptive potential to vault smaller, local businesses into powerhouse international companies.

It started with the three seeds of reinvention I'd found in my own history: I wanted to be outside the mainstream, challenged enough to remain deeply engaged, and involved somehow in food. Check, check, check. It was completely aligned with my core purpose: to support entrepreneurs. I had the currency to do it—maybe not the strongest currency in the world, but unique for Canada.

Now for the final step: assessing the market. This is something I do for clients all the time, so, luckily, I knew how to go about it (add that to my currency!). It's never a fishing expedition. You don't start by saying, *Let's find out what's hot right now, then reverse-engineer something that fits the bill.* Rather, you begin with a thesis and use research to test its validity.

My thesis was that there had been such a fundamental cultural shift in our attitudes about food that small, innovative companies were now disrupting the food industry—and, therefore, had become great investments. I could see evidence everywhere. There was so much noise about 100-mile diets, eating local, eating organic and food traceability, and so many conversations on social media tilted to the connection between food and health. My own taste preferences had changed dramatically, and I knew I was not alone.

The intersection between what we consume and our physical health had converged to the point where average consumers were becoming hyper-vigilant. At lunch and dinner meetings, I noticed that people who had never shown much interest in food were now interrogating the wait staff about ingredients. Phrases like "non-GMO" and "gluten-free" were suddenly on everyone's lips, and yet another cold-pressed juice company had opened within blocks of our office. At my local grocery store, there was minimal traffic in the canned food aisle, while artisanal, locally made products were flying off the shelves. And every article I read about food pointed to global concerns: pesticides in our produce, harmful chemicals in heavily processed food, the obesity epidemic, the safety of our food supply, how much better organic farming is for the environment, and on and on.

I'd come a long way since the days when I tried to pitch my idea of consolidation, though. I knew that investors weren't going to fork over millions of dollars based on my hunch. I'd need a raft of cold hard facts to persuade them to trust me with their money.

Fortunately, there was research showing that innovative food, beverage and health companies had indeed begun to disrupt the industry, because consumer preferences and behaviour had changed dramatically. In surveys, both millennials and boomers said they want to know where their food comes from and how it's made; they strongly prefer companies that are socially and environmentally responsible, and products that are produced sustainably with traceable ingredients. Because of this, health-conscious niche brands that are committed to transparency had been stealing market share away from the huge, established food companies. It used to be impossible for the little guy to muscle past the dominant brands and find a place on grocery store shelves, but companies had figured out how to sell their stuff online and in specialty shops, bypassing grocery chains altogether.

It was a David and Goliath story, and the Davids were winning. In North America, billions of dollars of food sales had shifted from large to small companies. Micro-brands—the type of companies I was looking to support via the accelerator—were going gangbusters, with sales growth almost five times that of large, globally recognized brands. The biggest players in the food industry weren't losing market share to each other but to the little guys and underdogs. Consequently, global food companies had begun to invest in and acquire innovative start-ups, both to head off the threat they posed and to diversify their own product offerings.

The context, in other words, could not have been more conducive for a VC fund focused on consumer goods in the food and beverage, health and wellness sectors. With the right support, I was convinced that these businesses could grow exponentially. The fact that they were Canadian was a big plus: Canada has a strong agricultural and manufacturing base, and our products are trusted around the globe.

In my head, I was already halfway to raising $100 million for this VC fund, so I went and talked to Ron Duke, who was the chief financial officer of Venture for many years, and whose opinion I trust. Ron thought the idea was a good one, but his background is in accounting, which means that being cautious is part of his DNA. He told me that raising a fund would be a lot harder than I imagined (he was right), and reminded me that Canadian investors are conservative and tend to instinctively resist new ideas (he was right). But he understood my desire to create a legacy and to use my own personal currency in a new way. So he rattled off all the challenges I'd face, and then he championed the idea, introducing me to lawyers who could put together what's called an Offering Memorandum. It's a bafflingly legalistic document you give to potential investors in a fund, and it costs a fortune to create. You *really* have to believe in your idea to pay for one of these things.

And by now, I did. I'd done my homework. I was ready to bet on my own idea. I hoped investors would be too.

External validation

Research has never been easier than it is in the digital age. There are mountains of information just a click away, and if you put in the time, you can gauge the market for your reinvention pretty easily. Ready to have a baby all on your own? You can research everything from sperm donors to child care options to single parents' support groups, without ever leaving home. Want to be a teacher? You can find out everything from the cost and location of the most innovative training programs to the median salaries in school districts around the globe. Want to know if the field of microbiology is growing or shrinking because of technological change? Google it, and you'll also come across the biggest controversies in the field and the hotbeds of academic research.

Even if you're 100 percent certain that market conditions are perfect for your reinvention, do your due diligence. Here's why: research is a form of external validation that will build your confidence—and trust me, you're going to need all the confidence you can muster. We all know the Disney script in which you just follow your dream, even when all forces are arrayed against you, and miraculously everything works out fine in the end. Cue the sunset. Maybe some people really do trip happily after their dream while bluebirds circle, but usually the story is a little grittier. Certainly it was for me. If I had $100 for every person who told me that raising a VC fund in the food sector was a terrible idea, I'd have met my financial goal in no time. Having facts at my fingertips reminding me that this was not a terrible idea at all was crucial, both to bolster my own confidence and to persuade other people that I knew what I was talking about.

Even when your intuition is screaming "go," you need solid data to prove to yourself and others that you're on the right path. Here are a few of the concrete indicators that boosted my own confidence en route to my reinvention: loyalty from my team, hard numbers and analytics pointing to a significant shift in the food sector, and the track record of the small food companies I'd already invested in. I was confident not just because of some hoo-ha inner feeling but because of the solid intelligence I'd gathered and my own track record as an investor.

If you're trying to do something where there's no precedent, it can be hard to find measures of external validation. We talk a lot in marketing about being "nimble" or "reactive" by following trends, but sometimes a reinvention is about identifying an empty space that has never been occupied. You're not chasing what's out there; you're trying to create what isn't. There may be few market indicators to gauge its potential.

In that case, then, you really need to understand the broader cultural context and how your idea fits into it. But frankly, I think this is important for any kind of reinvention. In the social media age, when we curate our newsfeeds and surround ourselves with voices similar to our own, we risk imprisoning ourselves in an echo chamber, sealed off from everyone who isn't like us. There might as well be a sign on the door: New Ideas and Perspectives Not Wanted. But in order to understand what's going on in the world, and to develop an awareness of cultural shifts and trends, you *need* exposure to different ideas and perspectives.

And because we live in the social media age, it's really easy to get that kind of exposure. Check out news sources you'd never usually consult, or follow someone on Twitter whose perspective is radically different from your own. If you're young, follow someone old, and vice versa. If you're conservative, see how a dyed-in-the-wool liberal views the world—don't just assume you know already. Talk to someone you know you'll disagree with, and instead of reflexively refuting her, point for point, really listen to what she's saying and consider her viewpoint objectively. Seeking out different perspectives doesn't mean you have to embrace or even agree with them. It just means that you are opening yourself up to understanding the world, not just your own small corner of it.

And that's good, no matter what type of reinvention you're about to attempt, because the next step is all about the rest of the world. You're about to go public.

Part Four

LIFE CHANGING

You've laid the groundwork. Now comes the part that requires a serious blast of courage: Stating your intentions. Out loud. To someone else. And then acting on them.

When I decided to leave *Dragons' Den* after eight seasons, I knew in my heart that it was the right decision for me. I'd really thought it through, and I was absolutely certain I was going to pull the trigger. But I hadn't told anyone at the CBC, or even hinted at it. I was at a conference in Hawaii when I realized that I really needed to stop planning my departure and actually depart. I had a little downtime between sessions, and had gone for a walk on the beach. *I'll do it tomorrow*, I promised myself, watching the waves roll in. Then I checked the time on my phone: forty-five minutes till the next session would start. I was putting my phone back in my pocket when I realized that there was no reason to keep putting this off. If I was so sure, what was I waiting for? I called a senior executive at CBC right there on the beach, as shorebirds scuttled in and out of the water looking for food, and told her I was leaving the show.

Now, you can think, *I'm quitting*, but until you say it out loud, it isn't real. As soon as the words came out of my mouth, all the equivocating and uncertainty dropped away. Until I heard myself quitting, I didn't fully believe I was going to do it. As soon as I did, it was like gears shifting in a car—I felt as though I'd suddenly jolted forward. I was on my way.

Saying it out loud is the bridge between intention and reinvention. It takes courage, honesty and introspection to plan your reinvention, but you need confidence to get past the planning stage and make it real by announcing your plan to the world.

And you *really* need confidence to stick to your plan and keep going when the going gets tough. Which it will. At some point, even if your reinvention involves leaving a bad job or a lousy relationship, you will almost certainly feel discouraged. Or exhausted. Or just ready to have an easier time of it. At those times, there's a strong temptation to throw in the towel or at least scale back your plan. This is when you need to dig deep, remind yourself of your core purpose and focus on preventing regret. If you stop before giving it your all, I can promise you that you will regret it. I know I have, every time I've scaled back on my dreams because achieving them felt so difficult and I wasn't sure I could do it.

To persevere, you need confidence both in yourself and in the soundness of your plan. That's one reason I've been suggesting you make notes and keep lists, so that you have a written record of your thinking and the progress you've made. Use it to bolster your confidence. In moments of weakness, look back at your time audit. Can you believe how much time you were wasting, or were frittering away on activities that didn't engage you and weren't related to your core purpose? Do you really want to fall back into that rut? Consult your list of your own currency too. You'll see that you have what it takes to keep going. You just may need to remind yourself frequently, and for some reason that's easier to do when you see your strengths enumerated on a piece of paper, in black and white.

Confidence is the fuel you'll need as you begin to talk the talk and walk the walk of reinvention. The streets may not be lined with people cheering you on. In fact, you may get a few rotten tomatoes lobbed your way (more on that in a minute). But you need to keep going until you reach your final destination: a better life. You owe it to yourself. And you can do it.

Chapter 8

Say it out loud

At Venture, when we're ready to tell the world about a brand reinvention, the strategists take all the background information they've gathered and the strategy they've developed to reposition the brand, and they distill it into a one-page brief for the creative team that actually creates the ads. The brief breaks down a messy blob of information into a simple, logical story: why the reinvention is occurring, who needs to know about it and what they need to know. If we gave the creative team hundreds or thousands of pages—which is usually how much information we've amassed from brand studies, research reports, focus group reviews and market data—they wouldn't have a clue what to focus on. The brief is called "brief" for a reason. It's a thumbnail sketch, not an endless Russian novel.

You want to inspire the creative team, not confuse them or bore them to death, so you're trying to give them a clear idea of the greatness of this reinvented brand. After all, their ability to promote it is dramatically improved if they believe in it themselves. Their role is to come up with the words and images that bring the brand to life for consumers—the ads you see in bus shelters and on TV, the content on the company's website. They're storytellers who excel at getting people's attention and communicating a brand's identity in a simple, smart and memorable way. When they do their job well, people who see the ad will play back exactly what we intended to communicate. *You thought this was a boring family car, but it's actually sporty, stylish and fun to drive.*

That's a pretty simple message, so you may be nonplussed at this point. Shouldn't people inside the company have been able to come up with that on their own? After all, they know their product better than anyone. But oftentimes, they're just too close to it. Either they can't clearly articulate what's special about their product—or they want to tell you every last thing about it. Think of those ads that run at 2 a.m., frantically reeling off thirty different things a vegetable chopper can do. When the ad ends, you can't remember a single one, but you're now suspicious that it's a cheap piece of junk: what kind of kitchen apparatus can be used for thirty different purposes, anyway?

Even great companies that make truly valuable products often just don't know how to communicate about them with outsiders. We saw this recently with a company in a very hot, high-growth sector that was already worth hundreds of millions of dollars. The leaders had big plans to scale to a billion-dollar company, but—and this is why they came to Venture—they had no succinct way to tell people what they had built. The CEO was committed; he clearly believed in the company's potential, but he couldn't explain what it was in any way that was inspiring or persuasive (or even comprehensible, to be perfectly honest). The company was great at operations. Hopeless at communication.

It might shock you to know how often we see this scenario. Sometimes people are super-excited about and proud of what they've built, and simply assume that everyone else will be too. When we ask, "Okay, but why? Why should someone else be excited?" they get defensive. "Well, isn't it obvious? I mean, I just told you: it's very exciting!"

As soon as I heard the CEO fumble for the words to describe his company and what they do, I knew that the momentum that had carried them this far wouldn't last forever. A leader has to be able to articulate what's special about a company in a way that everyone can understand. But landing on a succinct "elevator pitch"—one you can deliver in a thirty-second trip from the ground floor to fifth—requires a lot of introspection. Think of all the work you've just done: reviewing your history, determining your core purpose, taking stock of your currency and figuring out your context. Often the CEO and everyone else are way too busy just taking care of business to do all of that.

Our role as marketers, then, is to help them do it. We distill complex information, editing and refining it into a brand anthem that's crisp and clear enough that anyone who hears it will say, "Oh, I get it." Finding a sentence or phrase that crystallizes what a product is all about is worth a ton of money to a company, because consumers will never remember everything you tell them, but the right tag line may wind up indelibly engraved in their minds.

"Just do it." "Because you're worth it." "The real thing." The simpler, the better.

Your communications plan

It's easy to understand why a company wants and needs to communicate about its reinvention. But why should you? Who should you tell, and what should you say? The answers depend in part on what you're trying to do.

If you're looking at a job change or career shift, communicating that fact is not optional. You will need to talk about your plan in order to network, and executing will involve a wide range of other types of communication: your resumé, your profile on LinkedIn, your elevator pitch, what you say in interviews to explain why you're making this change—and all of it should line up under a consistent message. You need to communicate what's unique about you, and why you're changing course, in a simple, memorable way. "I hate my current job" won't cut it, even if it's your main motivation.

You know where I'm headed, right? Following the same process we use in marketing—figuring out your target audience and what moves them, settling on your key message and what you want people to remember, and coming up with a succinct way to describe yourself—is an excellent idea. You don't actually have to write a one-page brief, because these are instructions you're giving yourself, not a creative team. Nevertheless, I strongly advise it. The discipline of distilling complex information into a single page is incredibly helpful in terms of keeping yourself on track. You're forced to come up with a key message, so you'll never have to wing it in an interview or find yourself babbling incoherently when someone asks why on earth you're switching fields or companies. Being very clear on the "why" of your reinvention, so clear that you can express it in a sentence or two, will also have another benefit: it will increase your self-confidence.

But let's say that your reinvention involves going back to school to study physics part-time after you retire next month, and the starting point is a class at a community college. It may seem overly dramatic to go out and announce to the world that you have plans two mornings a week. You don't have to take out a full-page ad in the local paper, but you should definitely tell people what you're up to, for the same reason that I did have to call someone at CBC and resign. Until you state your intention out loud, you still have a lot of wiggle room. You can talk yourself out of it, or come up with a million reasons why you should wait to do it. Once the words are out of your mouth, though, you will feel a sense of obligation to follow through, if only to avoid looking foolish or lazy. When you talk about your plan, you're making it real in your own mind and other people's, which introduces accountability to the equation. If you never get around to enrolling for the class, people will ask, "Hey, whatever happened to that course you were going to take?"

If you're thinking that a personal reinvention of this nature doesn't really require a brief, you're right. But you should write one anyway, because the discipline of distillation is helpful regardless of the nature of the changes you're making. It clarifies your thinking, and that will pay dividends when you swing into action. Whenever you're making changes, people will be curious. Being able to explain to someone who couldn't care less about physics why you're excited to go sit in a stuffy classroom with a bunch of twenty-year-olds will reinforce your certainty about the path you've chosen and your confidence that you're ready to walk down it.

And there's another really good reason to broadcast a reinvention: you should be damn proud of yourself. Changing your life is courageous, and you should be proud to tell people that you've got the guts to do it. I think this is especially true if your reinvention involves a loss—of your job, say, or your relationship—or is being thrust upon you or if you feel defensive about it for some reason. Owning it is the first step to short-circuiting shame, as I found when I had to go into my office and tell everyone that my marriage was over but the president of the company and I were going to soldier on and continue working together. It was not a career highlight, to be sure, but simply saying it out loud diluted my sense of embarrassment a bit.

Shame will corrode your confidence like nothing else, which is why you can't let it take root at the very moment when you most need confidence. You don't have to give a blow-by-blow account of the dissolution of your marriage or being fired from your job, and in fact you shouldn't. Save that for a really close friend or your therapist. Ruminating over what's happened with all and sundry will not make you feel better anyway; it will ensure that you can't stop thinking about it or talking about it. You want to, and need to, focus on the next chapter. A simple declaration is best: "I was let go from my job, and I've decided to become a massage therapist because I really love making people feel better." You're signalling clearly that you're focused on the future, you have a plan that you're excited about, and you're really not interested in rehashing what went down.

Enlisting support

When you do announce your intention out loud, you may be pleasantly surprised by how much support you receive. As with a successful ad campaign, where people wind up humming the jingle, some people will embrace and applaud what you're doing. This is true whether you announce that you're starting a food truck or leaving your marriage.

As I mentioned, I did not publicize Venture's difficulties when the company was in serious trouble, but I did reveal our precarious situation to a few close friends and family. Then, once we'd committed to reinvention, I called an acquaintance who had started a successful business software company in the early nineties, which subsequently collapsed after 9/11 wiped out the financial services sector. Forced to cut his staff, he had weathered a crisis not unlike mine. With great determination, he'd started over. Within a few years he had revived his company, complete with higher-than-ever profits, before exiting with a multi-million-dollar sale. He'd since moved on to even bigger and better things.

While I respect this man immensely, we are not close friends. More neutral figures are often the best ones to talk to in times of crisis, though. A spouse or best friend doesn't always have a clear, objective take, and in any event, it's really helpful to talk to other people who have undertaken reinventions when you're embarking on one yourself. It doesn't matter if they're not in your industry or in your situation; they can probably still give you relevant information and advice.

This guy was in an entirely different sector, but he certainly knew about rebuilding after your company has taken a huge hit, and I knew, therefore, that he would never tell me to throw in the towel (remember: avoid toxic people!). He was both a great sounding board and a source of external validation. With him and a few others, I ran through all the different possible permutations: What's the worst-case scenario here? And the best-case? What's most likely to happen, and what should I watch out for? Just being able to talk to someone who had been there, done that, lifted the veil of stress and helped banish the shame of failure that had weighed so heavily on me after the flood.

He helped me identify the steps I needed to take. They were often difficult, and I remember thinking that it was like walking through mud. Eventually, though, as I kept moving forward—sometimes almost imperceptibly, other times in leaps and bounds—the mud got less thick and a little easier to walk through. I learned that Venture could be reinvented and so, in one important respect, could I: I didn't have to hide all my feelings. I'd discovered a better form of self-protection, namely, sharing them with people who could help me turn my company, and my life, around.

Sometimes, your message will fall on deaf ears

Not long after we began to rebuild Venture, I had my first exploratory meetings about the venture capital fund I was trying to raise. My goal was to raise $100 million, but that provoked such universal, incredulous laughter that I learned that was one thing *not* to say out loud. Instead, I'd tell potential investors that I planned to raise at least $25 million (but silently, in my head, I'd add, *plus another $75 million*). When you're raising a fund, you have to have skin in the game—if you're not prepared to risk your own money, why should anyone else?—and it's usually about 1 percent of the total amount you're trying to raise. I put in a million dollars, which is not an inconsequential amount of money for me or anyone else, because I really did believe I could raise another $99 million.

I was extremely lucky that *Dragons' Den* had raised my profile, so I booked a lot of meetings right away. Most of them, however, went nowhere. I could tell how quickly I was going to hit a dead end by how soon the conversation turned to the Den. Some potential investors didn't even bother feigning interest in the fund, and a lot of doors slammed in my face after people had achieved their objective: face time with the ex-Dragon.

Asking for money was awkward and unsettling at first—I was used to being the one giving the yes or the no, not the one doing the dog-and-pony show. But hey, at least I now knew for sure that I was an entrepreneur!

I quickly learned that persuading other people to give you their money so that you can invest it in early-stage companies in return for an equity stake is really, really difficult. There's significant risk with any VC fund, because a lot of promising early-stage companies gain momentum only to crash and burn—in which case investors lose every penny. We've all seen the headlines about the spectacular implosion of "surefire" early companies such as Theranos, the blood-testing start-up, whose investors lost many hundreds of millions of dollars. It's not surprising, then, that a lot of people who are happy to sink their hard-earned money into established companies and long-term investment funds might not touch a VC fund. Nothing ventured, nothing lost.

I needed to find institutions and high-net-worth individuals with an appetite for risk who were willing to bet on my judgment and my ability to spot winners in the food and health sectors—really, to bet on *me*, and the strength of my team. That's a tall order, because most investors who are comfortable with risk were (and still are) gung-ho on technology, not food. Huge food conglomerates were (and still are) floundering. It required a major leap of faith to believe that a company hatched in someone's kitchen could succeed when massive companies were on their knees. The fact that I had great research confirming the growth potential of that part of the food sector didn't sway many people.

A lot of folks just seemed to view food as a kind of dumb investment. Years ago, Warren Buffett said something I've never forgotten: "The business schools reward difficult complex behaviour more than simple behaviour, but simple behaviour is more effective." Sure enough, some naysayers gave my fund a pass, explaining patiently that food was . . . rather simple. They were looking for exciting, technology-driven investments, and if they involved artificial intelligence, even better. After I heard this for the twentieth time, I reminded myself that there's no way they knew more than Warren Buffett, who, early on, invested in food companies, calling them "the inevitables." He knew that, come what may, people will never stop needing to eat and drink.

His necessity-is-the-mother-of-investment approach made complete sense to me. But in the venture capital space in Canada, I seemed to be alone in that view.

Rely on the feedback loop

I couldn't just ignore the feedback I was getting. But I didn't have to interpret resistance as proof that my idea was dumb, either. I chose to see it as evidence that I needed to double down and think even bigger if I wanted to persuade people to partner with me. I wouldn't just pick the companies to invest in—I'd also roll up my sleeves and leverage all my currency, especially my marketing expertise and network, and Venture itself, to help them grow.

I'd build that ecosystem I'd been dreaming about, and beside it, in a kind of parallel universe, would be Venture, focusing on larger entrepreneurial companies. The ecosystem would include the VC fund and a business accelerator, a place where young companies with great ideas could get intensive expert help. I started recruiting mentors, food and wellness executives who were willing to volunteer their time at this not-yet-existent accelerator. They'd show entrepreneurs how to increase their sales and distribution, how to develop global strategies, how to manage a rapidly expanding business.

Most importantly, given my own currency, we'd provide extensive marketing and branding help, which is absolutely critical to helping food companies scale. You can have the best tomato sauce in the world, using your grandmother's secret recipe, but you won't sell cases of the stuff unless a lot of dominoes line up just so. You need a great brand identity, sustainable and attractive packaging, a great logo and website, a social media presence. You need to know how to use Instagram and Twitter to sell your sauce, how to get traditional retailers to carry it, and how to get bloggers and influencers raving about it. Your son can't manage all that on his laptop from your basement. You need people with real expertise and a track record. People like professional marketers.

When I first floated this idea, a few people suggested I use my own name, or Dragon-ness, to brand the whole thing. But that just felt wrong to me. This wasn't an exercise in self-aggrandizement. It wasn't about me, but about the small companies we were going to help—and rebuilding Venture. I decided to use the brand equity of Venture and call the ecosystem, which would include the VC fund, District Ventures. There are entertainment districts, finance districts, red-light districts—well, this would be a food/beverage and health district, a place where entrepreneurs would work, learn, eat and collaborate. The other thing I liked about the name was that consumers are increasingly concerned about knowing where their food comes from—which district.

I tried out the idea on the team at Venture, explaining that District Ventures would include its own dedicated marketing team, completely separate from Venture and devoted solely to helping the early-stage companies enrolled in the accelerator. A few hands shot up. "Can we please go over and do that? Please?" The prospect of getting in on the ground floor and trying to build a little company into a massive one was appealing to them for the same reason it is to me. It's an opportunity to be creative, make a big difference and really see the mark you're making. We brainstormed about all the things we could do to get District Ventures up and running: create an online hub, and maybe add a commercial kitchen so that entrepreneurs had a place to try out new ideas? And then we figured out how to pitch the whole sprawling, multi-tentacled thing that would include Venture plus the District Ventures accelerator and fund—what was it, exactly? *A one-stop entrepreneurial ecosystem.* Pretty good tag line, right?

Right away, it was obvious there were going to be some major challenges ahead. Funding this ambitious vision and rebranding ourselves as an entirely new kind of marketing entity were at the top of the list. But that's okay. Saying an idea out loud pulls back the curtain on the quality of the idea, revealing issues and potential roadblocks. They're not deal-breakers, they're just good indications of what you need to work on next.

The point I want to emphasize here is that I decided to do all this, which boiled down to quadrupling my workload and my stress level, not because I'd succeeded and raised a fund, *but because I hadn't.* Yet. Instead of backing off, I decided to ramp up and do more, offer more. As I mentioned, I do appear to thrive on uphill battles, and the steeper the grade, the more I seem to like it. I was running from meeting to meeting, fuelled by a potent combination of rock-solid conviction and high-octane stress, but I felt more energized than I had in a very long time. I always root for the underdog—I was one, for my first fifty years or so—and it was exciting to think about helping smaller companies go up against the giants of the industry.

There was something else going on too. The way I felt about myself was changing. Not because I was winning—I wasn't—but because I was *trying something entirely new*, and that was giving me a new way to look at myself and at the rest of the world. At a point in my life when I was supposed to be slowing down, I was speeding up and hitting new firsts: first fund, first accelerator, first ecosystem of its sort, first experience disrupting the venture capital model in Canada. I felt a new kind of confidence, exhilarating and meaningful.

I started talking up our reinvention whenever I got a chance. It took courage to tell other people what we were trying to do, but it got easier and more and more enjoyable, because my confidence kept growing with each scrap of encouragement. Each time I got an encouraging response—"Oh, that's a great idea. Why hasn't anyone ever done a fund and an accelerator for food before?"—I would tuck it away in a corner of my mind.

All that positive feedback provided a kind of inoculation against the indifferent or hostile responses that are to be expected when you announce that you're going to do something that hasn't been done before. I've heard Guy Laliberté, the founder of Cirque du Soleil, and Jim Balsillie from Research In Motion talk about the skepticism they faced at first, because what they were pitching was brand new. When Elon Musk announced, "I'm going to make an electric car," for the first time, people probably looked at him and said, "What are you even talking about? No one can fight the big auto manufacturers! It can't be done!" Pitching my food and health fund, I had to contend with similarly dismissive remarks: "Well, if it's such a big opportunity, Arlene, then why hasn't it been done before?"

The more I pitched, though, the more real the fund began to seem to me. Like the brief it's based on, a pitch serves a crucial psychological function. You're not just telling the world what you're going to do; you're making a promise to yourself, over and over, each time you say it. You're going to do this thing. No matter what.

Being first at anything is tough. If there's no precedent, you look like a risk, or a crazy dreamer. But when people discouraged me, it turned out to be helpful. I'm not kidding. It lit a fire under me to get out there and prove them wrong. And when the discourager was someone close to me, it was a good reminder to keep my distance.

Choose your fellow travellers wisely

As you embark on a sea change, it's important to look around and decide who's wanted on the voyage. Any frenemies should already be long gone. But everyone else who's still on board should be firmly on your side. Firmly and unequivocally. You need people around you who believe in you even when you don't. Their encouragement will help you stay the course.

In the past thirty years, I've run a marketing firm; I've been a venture capitalist; I've been on TV shows. While my core values have stayed the same, one thing has changed frequently: the people around me. I have a few anchor people in my life who provide me with a lot of joy, and our shared history matters to me very much. But I can't imagine what my existence would be like if my only friends were the ones I made when I was eighteen. The fact is, the friend you had wings with every Friday in your twenties may not be the one who will understand your struggle to start a new career in your forties. I think we're too hard on ourselves about this reality. Not all relationships will survive one party's overhaul. What's the most common reason people break up and friendships splinter? "I changed and he/she didn't—and didn't want me to, either."

Sometimes you need the people around you to change and evolve at the same time as you are changing and evolving, and sometimes they do. That can create a magical kind of synergy, where the whole becomes greater than the sum of its parts; a bond can be cemented forever when the two of you share a struggle, even if your ultimate goals are very different.

But over time, some relationships simply wear out, as may become obvious once you announce that you're heading in a new direction. You'll be thinking in a new way, experiencing new emotions, exploring new worlds; cracks in a relationship can quickly become unbridgeable chasms if someone else isn't willing to accept and support the ways that you're changing. That doesn't mean you should continue marching down your new path without so much as a backward look over your shoulder. Trying to change your life doesn't give you licence to behave like a jerk. You can still conduct yourself with kindness even while editing your social circle. You only need to remain committed to your new reality, whether it's trying to climb the corporate ladder, going back to school, staying at home full-time with your kids or starting your own business.

Distill the message

So here's an exercise for those of you who've decided that you're not going to waste time writing a brief. Test-drive your reinvention by announcing what you're planning to do to a couple of people you trust. Watch what happens when you try it out on your partner, your best friend, your father. Does your explanation ramble on and on? Is it loaded with "ands" or "buts" or bogged down by industry jargon? When you've finished talking, what's the look on the faces of people who care about you? Excitement? Dread? Confusion? You're not test-driving your reinvention just to get a reaction to the idea itself (external validation); you're saying it out loud so that you can hear it in your own ears (internal validation). Once you hear it, it becomes real, and open to improvement, if need be.

It is entirely possible that when you state your intention, it will sound ridiculous or ill-considered even to you. That doesn't mean you've failed. It means you need to step back, reflect, and, yes, you may want to write a brief. Tease out the story you want to tell. Make it cleaner, narrower, more concise. Whether your reinvention is dialing back professionally to focus on your family or taking a sabbatical to build homes in Peru, you have to be able to convey why it matters if you want other people to support you. If you can't, then there's probably a flaw in the plan that will trip you up eventually. But once you've landed on a good "pitch," your idea really will start to become a reality—to you and everyone around you.

I'm not talking about some New Age fantasy straight out of *The Secret*, in which positive thinking will magically yield a parking space or a boyfriend. I'm talking science: neuroscientists have found that when you say something out loud, your brain conjures a mental picture of what you're saying. Verbalization, then, begins to make something abstract into something concrete: you can actually see it as you say it. And the more times you say it, the more clearly you can see it, and the more real it becomes.

How you say it matters, though. There's a boatload of research to suggest that "the confidence gap" between men and women is real. Studies show that in the workplace, women don't speak up as much as men do, or negotiate raises for themselves as effectively as their male counterparts. Many women won't apply for a job unless they're 100 percent qualified, whereas men will fire off an application if they meet only 60 percent of the criteria on the posting. Knowing all this, one friend of mine braces for every negotiation with her own mantra: "Go in there like a man!"

But trying to exude hearty manly-man confidence can come off forced and phony (even from a man), and sound like empty bravado rather than hard-earned self-assurance. You'd know exactly what I mean if you could hear some of the voice mails I get. "Hi, Arlene! I've invented a brilliant new board game, and you're going to want a piece of it. Get back to me ASAP, while there's still time." "Hey there, Dragon Lady! I want to market my awesome handbags, which will sell themselves, but . . . that's really your shtick. So how about you sell them for me?" I'm flattered when entrepreneurs with good ideas reach out politely, but nothing turns me off faster than entitled swagger. When someone puts it on, it's usually a dead giveaway that their "confidence" isn't backed by competence. If your idea is viable, you don't need to posture or crow from the rooftops. If you really think you're on to something amazing, you look for backing and someone to partner with, not a coattail to grab on to, because you have confidence that your idea is strong enough to carry you.

It's pretty clear when people aren't really planning to reinvent but are looking to hand off their dreams so someone else can make them come true. But no one can make your dream come true except you, no matter how fantastic your idea is. A friend called me the other day to tell me she knows a woman who bakes really great pies, and she (and my friend) thought I should help her sell them, now that I had a food fund and all. Now, I happen to love pies—a little too much, probably! And I have no doubt that these ones are awesome. But, as I told my friend, I have never invested in a person who hasn't shown me that she would be perfectly fine without me. I need to know that if I say no, she's confident enough—and resourceful enough—to keep announcing her intention and scouting out opportunities until someone else says yes. I want to fuel a fire, not start one, and then have to stand over it, fanning the flames. Needing a little help is not the same as needing life support.

If you make the best pies in the world, believe in them enough to do the hard work of figuring out how to reinvent yourself as the owner of a pie company, then write your brief, craft your message and announce it to the world. I'm not the solution. Money isn't the solution. *You are the solution.* And true, lasting confidence, the kind that's required to remain on a new and unfamiliar path, comes only from knowing that you can start walking down it all by yourself.

Chapter 9

Launch

The day we launch a new brand or a brand reinvention is always exciting. The client is proud and a little nervous, and so are we. *We did it!* There's a flurry of activity and high-fiving, and sometimes some press attention too.

But then reality sets in, and the day-to-day work of reinvention begins. It can be a slog, even if what you're slogging toward is the most exciting and revolutionary thing on the planet. Usually, the world doesn't stop to applaud a reinvention. More often, there's resistance when you try to change the status quo. Our clients' competitors, for example, don't just roll over when we try to muscle in on their market share. Sometimes they come back punching, hard—undercutting our client on price, for instance, or unveiling their own marketing campaign bashing our client's brand.

Meanwhile, our clients are drumming their fingers on their desktops, anxiously awaiting results. Some expect to see them immediately: greater awareness of their brand, an uptick in terms of reputation, a spike in sales. Really large companies track these kinds of data daily or weekly, one of the decidedly mixed blessings of the digital world. The problem with being obsessed with the daily cash register data from your fast-food chain is that you may think nothing is happening though in fact something is. People may be aware of your new meatless burger and fully intending to give it a try—at some point. The fact that they didn't drop everything and run out to buy one the second you introduced it doesn't mean that the new product, or the marketing campaign for it, is a bust.

It may take time for consumers to believe that you've really changed. People don't just forget, overnight, that your brand used to be all about the beef. They need to see you in a new light for a while before they buy that, now, you're offering healthy fast food. And then it might take months, or even a year, for people to conclude that your vegetarian burger tastes great, and really is better than anyone else's.

In the meantime, we've got to keep telling the world, in different ways, all about that meatless burger and what wonderful things it says about your company. If we stop because people don't immediately start buying it, the brand reinvention will never have a chance to succeed.

In other words, reinvention is a process, a gradual one. People won't necessarily understand or accept right away that you're different now. You might get a quick bump from a really clever new ad campaign, but it's usually temporary. It almost always takes more than one ad, or one in-store promotion, or one logo change, or one update to a website. The company has to prove, over and over, in everything it does, that it has changed in some fundamental way. Patience and perseverance matter.

The same is true in a personal reinvention. You may quit your job, or leave your relationship, or move to Rome, and expect a whole new life to unfold, pronto. It probably won't, though, not right away. You've fired the starting gun, is all. Now you have to start running. Maybe it will be an all-out sprint. Maybe it will be a marathon. Whatever the case, you need to keep going and believe you'll reach the finish line eventually, even if you can't see it right now. You're just getting started. And you're racing against yourself, not time.

Pace yourself

After deciding to create District Ventures, I used my own funds to start hiring people to create the accelerator, then got back to pounding the pavement, looking for investors in the venture capital fund. Now I was really fired up with confidence about the idea, the approach and our team. I could easily picture the next fund being $250 million. I fully expected that I'd be getting started on that very soon. How long could it possibly take to raise $25 or $30 million and close the first fund?

I pitched my heart out when I met with representatives of various institutions and an assortment of high-net-worth individuals, and I also listened, to learn everything I could. Any new field has its own concepts, assumptions and shorthand, and I had to master them. It was exhausting, it was exciting, and I did get better as time went on. Jargon that had been unfamiliar to me at first now tripped off my tongue with ease. I found the right balance of warmth, authenticity and seriousness, which was important because people needed to like me enough to want to partner with me, and also trust that they'd get back at least as much as they invested. With some people, the fact that I'd been on TV was a plus. With others, it was a liability—some didn't seem to take me seriously as a business person, and treated me as though I'd just played one on the Den. After nearly three decades in the business world, that was a little annoying, and sometimes I wasn't sure if it really was the TV thing or my gender that was the issue.

But I also understood, because I'd seen it happen to some of our clients at Venture, that it can take time for other people to get their heads around a reinvention. They're used to seeing you one way, and their perspective may not shift just because you've waltzed in the door singing a new song. They have no clue how much work you've done to get to this point, or how committed you are to making this change. From their perspective, it's come out of the blue, with no warning. So they're skeptical.

A lot of prospective investors weren't just skeptical but actively discouraging. Either I wasn't the best person, or this wasn't a good idea, or the fund wasn't big enough, or the fund was too big, or I should come back when it was a proven success. That last point, which I heard more often than any other, is indicative of what I think of as a very Canadian attitude. It's one reason that *Dragons' Den* has been so successful: a lot of people who go out seeking investment for good business ideas are told to come back and ask again after they've made it big, which is why they wind up having to go on a TV show to find backing. Risk aversion in the investment community hurts Canadian entrepreneurs and, ironically enough, was exactly why I needed to start the accelerator and the fund in the first place: to help promising companies that can't get the capital they need to grow. Every day, I was receiving first-hand evidence of the need for a more robust venture capital system and less cautious investors, because people were unwilling to invest in me too.

I hadn't experienced that sort of rejection in years, and yes, it did start chipping away at my confidence. The fact that I'd been successful in other areas didn't fortify me. I had a big dream, and I was making little progress. Maybe the universe was trying to tell me something?

A year in, I had raised only $16 million (yes, I know that's an astonishing amount of money—unless you're talking about the capital required to propel multiple small businesses onto the international stage). On the glass-is-half-full front, I was more than halfway to my fund goal. Sure, it was going more slowly than I would have liked, but it wasn't an unmitigated disaster. On the glass-is-half-empty front, there was my inner critic, nattering away about how foolish I was going to look when I didn't meet my target.

I remember I came out of one dead-end meeting and I was just done. The self-talk was as loud as a jet engine: *Why aren't people jumping on this? What's wrong with this idea? What's wrong with me?* I felt as though I was letting everybody at Venture down. Again.

As I walked down the street, feeling dejected and frustrated, I called an adviser who knew the intricacies of what I was trying to pull off. "I don't think I can do this anymore," I told him. "It's just not working." I walked and complained, complained and walked, and finally he decided he had heard enough. "What are you talking about?" he bellowed into the phone. "You *are* making progress. You just can't see it right now because you're too close to it. Now quit complaining and get to the next meeting!"

I'm so grateful to that guy for the scolding. Here was someone I had a lot of respect for, who really understood what I was trying to do, telling me I was doing fine—with the exception of my attitude. I'd been worrying that I was letting him down, but apparently he believed in me—but not my attitude. He reminded me to stop being melodramatic and dig deeper, for a little courage. I did, and lo and behold, there it was.

This kind of moment is when all the work you did early on, figuring out who you are and what matters to you, really pays off. He gave me the kick in the ass that I needed, but I already had all the other ingredients: certainty about my core purpose, a list of my currency, solid understanding of the cultural context, and a real sense, for the first time in my life, of the connections between my past and present, as well as a very clear idea of the future I wanted. I just had to review all of that mentally, then buckle down and keep going.

We were launching the only business accelerator in the country specializing in food and health products. Building a one-stop shop for entrepreneurs was something no one else in Canada was doing. Tying a marketing agency, a venture capital fund, an accelerator and entrepreneurs together was a new model. Of course it was a hard sell! We were doing something new. The fact that I'm female, and so few women in Canada have raised VC funds, likely made it even more difficult for some prospective investors to see the value of the business proposition—but it bumped up my own resolve, too. I knew that if I failed, it would be that much harder for the next woman who tried to raise a fund. Those who go first have an obligation to make sure they're not also the last. I *had* to succeed.

I added that adviser to my "frequently called" contact list, knowing I'd probably be in need of another talking-to at some point soon, and marched off to my next meeting with my early-days confidence reignited.

Play to win, don't play not to lose

Shortly after I rededicated myself to my fund, I ran into a slightly nosy acquaintance whose expertise is investments. I tensed up, knowing that she would be asking, "So, what are you up to?" Sure enough, she did. And sure enough, I felt a rush of embarrassment: the fund wasn't building as quickly as I'd hoped, and now I would have to reveal that to this person. Great. I tried to separate out my embarrassment and focus on facts, simply telling her that I'd raised $16 million for my first VC fund. Unlike me, she didn't have all kinds of emotional baggage wrapped up in the number, so she was impressed. "That's a good-sized first fund. Do you know how few people ever make it that far in Canada? It's good enough! Why don't you stop there?" she asked, not unkindly.

But I was appalled. Sure, I'd had the thought myself, but when I heard someone else voicing it, it sounded like an insult, though I don't think it was intended to be. Here, at last, I had an opportunity to scale-up my ambition, use the currency I had earned and do what I love to do most of all: help other entrepreneurs realize their dreams. If I didn't keep going, I would be letting them, and myself, down in the worst possible way, to say nothing of what I'd be doing to the team at Venture. They were in the trenches too, trying to pull off this reinvention. I thought: *I have only so much time left on this earth, and it's got to be meaningful. Right now, this fund isn't big enough to be meaningful to Canadian entrepreneurs. It's going to take a long time and be really hard, but I'm going to get to at least $25 million, damn it!*

That "at least" was important, because I never let go of my goal of getting this first fund to $100 million. I really had to hold tight to that objective and tune out the chorus of voices telling me my dream was too big and my goals were too lofty, especially when I was $84 million short of my goal. I knew that if I pulled back, I'd be succumbing to what's called loss aversion: playing not to lose, rather than playing to win. Losing is painful, the theory goes, so some people will do just about anything, including quitting the game altogether, to avoid it. For them, anticipation of the pain that accompanies losing is an even more powerful motivator than the anticipation of an exhilarating win. If that was my mindset too, I'd never get to $25 million, much less $100 million.

That conversation with the $16-million woman was a turning point. When she innocently suggested dialing down my expectations, I knew instantly that I'd be filled with regret if I followed her advice. Even if I never raised another dollar and wound up having to close the fund at $16 million in five years' time, at least I'd know I'd given it my very best shot. I couldn't honestly say that yet, which made the path forward very clear: I just had to keep going. Inadvertently, she'd triggered my persistence.

I didn't want to settle. I wanted to build something great. I wanted to build a platform, not just a stand-alone fund. There's nothing embarrassing about not meeting your own unrealistic, self-imposed deadlines, unless you choose to be embarrassed. When my kids were little and learning to read, tie their shoes and ride bikes, I didn't go crazy on them when they didn't master a new skill in thirty minutes. I told them to be patient with themselves, to keep working at it, to view their mistakes as learning opportunities.

It's good advice. Expect missteps. Expect to spin your wheels occasionally. Expect missed deadlines. They don't mean you're worthless, or that your plan is pointless. They are proof that you're changing and learning, and both activities can be messy.

If you really feel like quitting at some point, ask yourself how you would feel later on if you pulled the plug. If you'd feel that you'd left something important unfinished, you have all the information you need. Keep going. Just be a little kinder and gentler with yourself while you do.

Critical cheerleaders

The path to success usually isn't straight or easy. You're flying down a flat road at a good clip, then the road bends and . . . Uh-oh. There's a mountain dead ahead, and it didn't appear on any of your maps. You have no choice but to figure out how to get up and over the thing.

You should anticipate that the change you're undertaking will take longer than you imagined, and be harder than you thought (worst-case scenario: I'm wrong, and you're pleasantly surprised). You should also anticipate that you are going to need support at some point, even if you're a lone wolf type or pride yourself on your self-reliance. Nobody ever truly "goes it alone." Even the strongest personalities and so-called self-made men and women need others to fill the holes in their own skill sets and offer smart, objective feedback. Also, reinvention can get lonely, especially if, as part of it, you've had to separate from your social circle. A little camaraderie can go a long way.

Before you launch your reinvention, then, it's a good idea to have a list of names and contacts in your back pocket: people who will provide a life raft, or light a fire under you, or remind you to keep putting one foot in front of the other. Most people *like* being asked to help, and will gladly give you at least a few minutes of their time, so long as you approach them with humility and respect. Even a relationship that's been off-line for a while can come back to life if you ask for a hand.

Coming up with some names now, before you're feeling desperate and discouraged, will provide a kind of quiet comfort—an insurance policy, if you will—along the way. I'm not talking about a list of yes-men and sycophants who think that everything you do is wonderful. At this stage of your reinvention, you'll need cheerleaders with a critical streak—people who want you to succeed and will therefore dole out tough love to make sure you do. These are the trusted advisers you need in your corner when you start to whine, sell yourself short or slack off, because they won't let you get away with it. Unlike frenemies, who try to tear you down to make themselves seem bigger, critical cheerleaders try to build you up. They're on your side. They know their role is to remind you why you decided to change your life in the first place, and hold you accountable for keeping your word.

If your reinvention involves work or business in any way, one reason you'll need a reliable sounding board is that there's a good chance not all the feedback you're going to receive will be entirely honest. There's a reason that Canadians are known for excessive politeness. Here, a no sometimes sounds like a maybe that you might be able to convert to a yes—but it's actually just a flat no. "We think it's a great idea," someone may tell you, with such a wide smile that you can't hear the implied "but."

Early on, I wasted a lot of time circling one particular institution that gave me a massive runaround, never quite saying no, then getting back to me with encouraging feedback, and then not getting back to me at all. It turned into a toxic relationship. For a full year I tap danced, trying to show that District Ventures was worthy of a yes, until I realized that we'd never even been close. Pigs would fly before these guys would invest a dime, but no one was ever willing to come right out and say that. They appeared to think that it was kinder to string me along and waste hours and hours of my time (and theirs).

I'd feel better about this experience if I knew that you'd learned from my mistake: remain skeptical when you hear what sounds like positive affirmation, and even ask, "Are you just trying to let me down gently, in which case I'd rather hear the unvarnished truth?" If there's a no lurking just beneath the surface, try to lure it out into the open, so you can move on if you have to. If you're not sure, ask a critical cheerleader for his or her take on the situation.

And no matter how bruising the rejections, keep moving forward. Even at the lowest moment, after I'd heard no after no, I still believed deep down that District Ventures made sense and was worth the time, effort and money I was putting into it. I just had to keep plowing ahead.

If your reinvention is of a more personal nature, it may be quite a bit more difficult to find a critical cheerleader. Sometimes, people just don't want to get involved, and they'll "yes" you to death. Other times, the critics may be all too happy to weigh in. "Leaving a twenty-year marriage because you're *bored*?! Honey, after twenty years, everyone is bored." "But why would you go back to school? It's not like you'll ever get a job as a lawyer at your age." "I get that you want to have kids, but adopting a twelve-year-old? That kid has been through so much, he's going to make your life a living hell. Sorry, but someone's got to say it."

Sometimes the criticism is ignorant but well-intentioned; sometimes it's just ignorant. In either case, don't let it rattle you. This is your life, to live as you wish. You've done your homework, and you know better than anyone else what's right for you. This isn't some cockamamie idea you cooked up one night after a few too many glasses of wine. This is a well-thought-out decision. You've already determined that you have the correct currency and you've also decided that you want your core purpose to serve as your guiding light from this point on.

Ignore the critics and consider looking for people who've already done whatever it is you're trying to do, who are familiar with some of the challenges you'll face. People who've been there, done that, may already know how lonely the journey you're embarking on can feel, and may be more than happy to walk a ways with you—and prod you onward, if necessary. You might have to cast your net wide to find them, but there are chat rooms and support groups for every imaginable situation, just a mouse click away.

Trainers

When you're doing something new, you are bound to make rookie mistakes. That's okay. You *are* a rookie. There's a learning curve, as there always is when you're trying to do something you've never done before. To climb up it, you may need some help from people who know the terrain better than you do.

If you're lucky, you'll meet people with expertise you don't have, who are generous enough to provide a little personal training. That's what happened to me a couple of years ago. I was waiting for a cab outside a hotel in Toronto, and so was an unassuming man in a long wool coat. Out of the blue, he turned to me and said, "Somebody told me you're famous. Who are you?" I was both put off and intrigued by his bluntness. "Well, who are you?" I shot back. It turned out he was Dino Trevisani, then the president and general manager of IBM Canada. Okay, well, I can recognize a business opportunity when one is standing outside a hotel.

We started talking, and he turned out to be sharp and funny. Far from being a corporate stuffed shirt, he's a pretty regular guy from Hamilton, Ontario. After years of being based in New York, he'd returned to Toronto because he wanted to boost innovation in his home country. No sooner did he say that than we started talking about what Canadian entrepreneurs really need in order to succeed, and the rapport was instantaneous. We weren't just on the same page—we were practically finishing each other's sentences.

I knew, of course, that IBM was a major investor in entrepreneurial incubators, so I told him about the new accelerator at District Ventures, which is a kind of living lab for promising new businesses in the packaged food sector. In exchange for a minority equity stake in these companies, we provide office space and a five-month boot camp, including expert, hands-on help with sales, distribution and marketing. But the piece I was most excited about was the mentoring. We put leads at these new companies together with established, experienced industry counterparts, who advise and guide the entrepreneurs.

I made the pitch: "We should talk about how IBM could be involved." Right there, on the sidewalk, about half an hour after clapping eyes on me for the first time in his life, Dino said, "Let's make it happen." This was in the early stages of our reinvention, and I'll tell you, getting the thumbs-up from Dino Trevisani gave my confidence a huge boost. Talk about external validation!

I also loved the fact that I'd be joining forces with a company with one of the greatest reinvention stories in business history. In order to survive for over a century, IBM has had to reinvent itself innumerable times. The company produced some of the biggest, earliest innovations in technology, from mechanical punch cards to the bar code. But when the personal computer revolution happened in the eighties, IBM was looking the wrong way, toward mainframes; they stumbled and lost the lead. By the early nineties, IBM was losing billions to Microsoft and Apple. But rather than pack it in, IBM reinvented as a consulting service, offering IT support to corporations around the world. IBM now earns most of its revenue in services, not products. The reinvention was so smart: they'd missed the personal computer moment, but rather than panicking and trying to catch up, they identified a new space that no one was yet occupying, and in they stepped.

Dino and I moved fast. We put our senior people together, and within a few months we had signed off on a partnership. Today, the District Ventures and IBM Innovation Space is tucked on the second floor of our new, post-flood offices in Calgary. It's an accelerator, but separate from the food accelerator; this one brings tech entrepreneurs and big enterprise together to solve business challenges. Large corporations can test an innovative business model or develop a product; entrepreneurs can access powerful technologies such as IBM's Watson to help them develop their own businesses, and they also have amazing mentors, including a number of CEOs of tech companies, as well as business development help. Best of all, corporate heavyweights and tech-savvy upstarts can collaborate on new, disruptive products and services. I love it up there, and not just because of the bright light streaming in and the colourful furniture (why would you live in the grey zone when there's so much colour in the world?). The energy at the boot camps makes me feel rejuvenated, as if I've just had a painless injection of B_{12}.

Venture and IBM had a shared interest in helping entrepreneurs thrive, but Dino had experience with technology start-ups and I did not. I needed his support—and also his push-back. As we built the incubation space, he told me things that were hard to hear, because they challenged my own thinking. I learned a ton working with him, knowledge that helped me build out the District Ventures food accelerator too, and secure a separate group of food and wellness executive mentors.

None of it would have happened, though, if I hadn't reinvented the way I interact with other people. And to do that, I had to change myself first.

Reinvented

Ten years ago, if Dino had tried to strike up a conversation with me on the street, I probably would have responded, polite Canadian that I am. But it would not have occurred to me to share my own goals, aspirations and convictions with him. I would have thought, *Oh, he runs IBM Canada, he doesn't want to hear me babble on about my little marketing firm.*

I remember being in a meeting in Ottawa in 2012 with Peter MacKay, then minister of national defence, the day I was appointed an Honorary Naval Captain. It was a high-powered group, and I was thrilled to be there. As the conversation turned less formal, I wanted to weigh in on a political issue that had been in the headlines that day. What an opportunity! I had the ear of a senior member of the government, which doesn't happen every day. But I hesitated, wondering whether my comment was smart enough, and while I was still mulling it over, someone else said *exactly* the thing I had been gearing up to say. Naturally, my inner critic went to town: *Why didn't you say it? You idiot! Well, of course, that guy runs a multi-billion-dollar company and Venture is dinky by comparison, so . . .*—and on and on went the tickertape, just as it had when I was an awkward teenager, looking at myself in the mirror and wondering if there was anything worthwhile about me at all.

By the time I met Dino, I had changed. To reinvent Venture, I'd had to reinvent myself. I'd had to put myself out there, again and again, state our goal and our purpose, and persuade myself and other people that I was capable of things I'd never tried to do before. To have the gumption to ask other people to believe in me, I'd first had to believe in myself—enough to overcome my shame and feelings of failure about Venture's near demise, and enough to weather uncertainty, rejection and the possibility of yet more failure. Along the way, I'd become both more confident and more humble, less afraid of making mistakes and less prone to beating myself up when I did. I felt more comfortable in my own skin and a whole lot better about myself, because I knew what my core purpose was, and I knew I was delivering on it.

So of course, when I met someone new, I happily told him what I was doing and asked if he wanted to help. I knew that the worst that could happen was that he'd say no, and I'd heard "no" so many times that it no longer scared or embarrassed me or induced an attack of self-doubt or self-pity. I was absolutely certain I was on the right path. If people didn't want to link arms and walk with me, I was fine with that. No hard feelings. I just had to keep going.

Reinventing feels like pushing a gigantic snowball uphill. It's tough: you're huffing and puffing, getting that snowball going, and then it rolls back and knocks you right over, so you have to start again. But with every push, you learn something. And then one day you and that giant snowball are at the top of the hill. Your reinvention actually worked, and you look down and think, *Nothing beats this feeling.* Success—however you measure it—is like your own personal Olympics. You trained and worked and sacrificed and dreamed, and it paid off. The sense of accomplishment is epic. But you're not done. Your next move isn't to plop down and slide back down the mountain on your rear end. The view from the summit is incredible, and one thing you see is the next mountain you want to climb. You want to experience that struggle, and that high, all over again.

Two and a half years after I started, I'd raised a first round of $30 million, but I had no intention of stopping there. Today, the fund stands at $70 million, District Ventures is up and running, and both accelerators are going full speed. Venture is on its own separate trajectory, working with clients who are further down the entrepreneurial road, and motoring along as though there was never any issue. We have 50,000 square feet dedicated to nurturing innovation and early-stage companies, including a brand new 20,000-square-foot commercial kitchen in Toronto where the companies we back can test new ideas and work on their products.

I'll never forget the moment I realized our reinvention was succeeding. I was sitting in a boardroom, watching the team pitch the first piece of business as the new, reinvented Venture. As soon as they started talking, with such passion and conviction, about being a one-stop shop for entrepreneurs, it dawned on me: *It's really happening!* The idea wasn't just in my head anymore; it was in the world, and my team was selling it confidently and clearly. I allowed myself a moment to savour the success, and then I rolled up my sleeves and pitched in. There was still work to do.

Putting it all together

The District Ventures accelerator has become one of my favourite places on earth. It's a kind of reinvention machine, where you get to see other people changing their lives in real time. In 2016 we had more than a thousand applications for our five-month program linking entrepreneurs with mentors and networking opportunities, but could accept only a handful of applicants. One pitch that stood out was Shelby Taylor's.

Shelby had been a journalist, but when newspapers and magazines downsized or folded altogether, as part of the digital media revolution, she knew she had to make a change. Nutrition had always been a personal passion—currency, in other words (see how an untapped interest can be spun into a reinvention?). So she bought a small health food store outside Collingwood, Ontario, on the coast of Georgian Bay. Retail wasn't her dream, but she did need to work and she liked being immersed in the health food industry. She also enjoyed talking to customers and distributors, gathering information about what they'd like to see on the shelves—figuring out the context, in other words. Talking to people, she heard over and over that mealtime with little kids was hell. She knew a thing or two about that herself, because she had a family too.

There were really two issues: time and taste. "Families were struggling to find the time to prepare a healthy meal," Shelby says. But when they did, guess what? Often, their kids refused to eat it. All they wanted was pasta, plain, which really isn't all that nutritious. Shelby's own health food store carried a couple of pastas made with pulses such as chickpeas and lentils, but they were blended with rice, they weren't organic, and they weren't exactly a taste sensation. So Shelby set her sights on producing a line of organic, gluten-free, super-nutritious pasta that kids actually liked and would eat.

How much formal training did she have in nutrition? Zero. How much experience did she have in manufacturing? Zero. But she did have some currency: her interest in food, her own experience as a mom, her recently acquired experience as the owner of a health food store, and her curiosity about the world, which became a superpower when she combined it with the interviewing skills she'd developed in journalism. Shelby is one of those people who is always asking questions, and she knew from grilling her customers that a pasta made solely from chickpeas and lentils would probably meet all their requirements. If only she could make it taste good.

She spent a year on product development, including a couple of months in a rented corner of the kitchen of an Italian restaurant, where she and her mother experimented with chickpea flour and a gigantic pasta extruder, trying to find the winning formula. When she finally did, she launched a Kickstarter campaign, seeking investors who could help provide the capital she needed to begin producing her pasta. She raised $27,000—external validation that a market existed.

All along the way, she was e-mailing and cold-calling suppliers, business teachers at the local community college and other entrepreneurs—anyone who might have a scrap of wisdom to impart about starting a food company. "I have never been afraid to ask questions. I'll call literally anyone," Shelby says. "I've talked to my biggest competitors, which is something everyone says you're not supposed to do. But why not? You have nothing to lose. What I would say to anyone who is reinventing is: ask questions. Learn from people who have been there. You learn so much just from asking people to tell you their stories." It's also a great way to acquire critical cheerleaders and trainers.

Like me. I was one of the people Shelby interrogated along the way, and it worked: I gave her a spot in the District Ventures accelerator because I believed in her and wanted to invest in her company, which she'd named Chickapea. Shelby's pitch stood out not just for the quality of her pasta but because she asked smart, pointed questions at the interview. She approaches people with such zippy, authentic curiosity that it's hard to say no to her.

A word about timing: when she applied to the accelerator, Shelby was pregnant with her second child. She did not use her pregnancy as an excuse to take a rain check, though. Hell-bent on reinvention, she leapt on the opportunity when we offered her a spot, and came to Calgary one week every month to take our courses, as do all the entrepreneurs who are located elsewhere in Canada. It's important for them all to be there at the same time, because one of the big benefits of the program is that they meet other people who are in exactly the same situation. They learn from and support one another—ideal fellow travellers, in other words.

Shelby was nine months pregnant when we were hammering out the details of our financial investment in her company, and there were many late night calls with our CFO to revise Chickapea's cash flow model and figure out all the details. Unfortunately, babies don't have a whole lot of respect for deadlines, and Shelby's arrived before the papers were signed. Two days later, she signed off on the District Ventures Capital investment with a newborn on her lap.

Which is to say: reinventing isn't easy. Shelby has struggled with guilt over what she might be missing at home as she balances an entrepreneur's long hours with the needs of a young family. But like so many people who are driven to change their lives for the better,

Shelby doesn't feel she has a choice. She *needs* to do this. "I do think I might be a little on the crazy side, but I also think you have one life to live and you've got to try," she said. "It's so much work. But if you're willing to work really, really hard and you're really determined, I'd tell anyone who was considering a reinvention to go for it. I have so many friends who can't wait for the weekend, while I'm at my desk on a Friday night and I have so much to do, but I'm so happy. You have to take big risks to get big payoffs."

As a former journalist, she has top-notch communication skills and knows how to write a brief and tell the world why she's making nutritious, high-protein, non-GMO food for families. Her pitch helped grow the company right over the border and into the United States. And now she has to ramp up production: her new vegan mac and "cheese" in a box, a 100 percent healthy version of Kraft Dinner that's made with creamy sweet potato and pumpkin sauce, sells out so quickly that she has difficulty keeping it in stock.

As her company has expanded, Shelby has found her core purpose, which sometimes reveals itself fairly late in the proceedings. One day, after her chickpea pasta had finally hit the shelves of specialty health food stores, Shelby got a message from the mother of a three-year-old. The little girl had severe allergies, and the dinner table had turned into a war zone. There was nothing this kid liked to eat that didn't make her ill and, consequently, she was alarmingly underweight. Everyone was worried sick about her. But when her mom gave her a bowl of Shelby's high-protein, organic pasta, she ate every last piece, then lifted up her empty bowl, asking for more. The mom broke down in tears, and so did Shelby when she read the message. "Getting that note," she said, "made all the struggles worth it."

It nudged her toward an important recognition: her mission isn't just to run a profitable business, but to do good in the world by helping people eat and live better. Her expectations for herself and her business continue to widen and deepen, to fulfill that core purpose. She is, for example, committed to creating products in an environmentally friendly way and making them available to all—which is why, from the beginning, she has been donating cases of Chickapea to food banks.

I could not be more proud to have had a hand in Shelby's success, and the success of the 75-odd companies that have graduated from the District Ventures accelerator program so far. We've helped them get off the ground and get their products onto shelves in thirty countries, and last year their revenues were approximately $65 million. That's good for them, good for us and good for the Canadian economy. The best news of all is that every day we are learning more about how to help early-stage companies create, manufacture, market and distribute their products, and scale-up to take on the big food conglomerates and disrupt the industry. The reinvention continues.

Your publicity campaign

Recently, a good friend of mine was giving a speech to a room filled with venture capitalists, private equity people and financial hotshots—heavy hitters, in other words. He'd invited me to sit at the head table. When we were all seated, a well-regarded, successful businesswoman went around the table introducing everyone: "This person accomplished this; that person accomplished that"— all very impressive. But when she got to me, she said, "And this is Arlene Dickinson, a guest of the speaker."

I was, to say the least, annoyed. I was the only woman at the event who had raised a fund. This was a room brimming with possible capital for that fund and potential connections and mentors for the companies we were nurturing at the accelerators. I wondered, *Have I done such a poor job of marketing our reinvention that no one knows what I've been up to?* Sometimes the baggage of who you were before your reinvention is hard to shed. People have an outdated version of you locked in their minds, sort of like the way our parents sometimes talk about us: "Oh, you've always been terrible at math." And you think, *Really? I was ten when I was terrible at math. Now I run a business, so I do know how to add.*

After a reinvention, you might have to undo an imprint of your former self that still exists in other people's minds. If the world continues to see you as you were before, your reinvention will feel incomplete. Perhaps you're now a singer, or the head of a start-up, or happily single—whatever your reinvention, you have to let people know about it. It takes time to undo a storyline and repaint a picture that people have created about you. There might be moments when you're sitting in a room and no one acknowledges who you are now, and that will be irritating. Luckily, there's a simple fix: tell them.

It's okay to insist (politely!) on acknowledgement. It's also smart: if you talk about what you've done, you'll attract those who are interested in building relationships and offering insight—expanding your network and solidifying your reinvented identity. You don't have to be a jerk about it. At that event, there was no need to climb on the table and shout, "Attention, everybody! I have a fund and an ecosystem for entrepreneurs!" But I did make sure, over the course of the evening, to connect with each and every person at the table and tell them what I've been doing for the past five years. When I talk about the reinvention of Venture, I focus on the hard work we did. (I don't like it when people shrug off their accomplishments and say, "Oh, it was nothing." Of course it was something! We should always be real about the hard work required to get somewhere.) Note the "we" there. It's important to give credit where it's due, and to acknowledge other people in the process.

Just as no one but you could imagine your reinvention, much less undertake it, no one else is going to trumpet your success. It's up to you. Don't shrink away from acknowledging what you've done—you have no idea who's listening, or who might be inspired, or who really needs to hear that it's possible.

On that note . . . By the time you read these words, the District Ventures fund should have reached or be very close to $100 million. We are building a platform, one that will make an enormous difference to individual entrepreneurs and to Canada, in a space with limitless potential. And speaking of limitless, I now have a new goal: to get the fund to $1 billion.

Before the flood, I never would have admitted such a thing out loud. My inner critic would have had a fit: *Who do you think you are?* I no longer ask myself that question, though. I don't need to, because I know the answer.

An entrepreneur. A reinventor. A woman who is just getting started.

Conclusion

My place north of Toronto is one of my favourite spots in the world, with a backyard that's more like a meadow, where black raspberries grow in the summer. Behind the house, mossy trees huddle in a little forest. The cottage is cozy and welcoming, not grand or fancy, and my favourite part is that a river rushes past it, creating a never-ending symphony of water on rocks.

When a warm spring arrived suddenly in 2016, all the winter ice melted at once and ran down into the river. The municipality made the decision to lower a nearby dam, with the intention of allowing more water to flow into Georgian Bay. It didn't quite work out that way. Instead, water from the dam combined with the melted ice, and the river started to rise.

I knew that the river was high, but I'd been checking online and there was no suggestion that a flood was imminent. I wasn't too worried. When I woke up on the weekend and looked outside, though, I thought, *Oh, no. Not again!* The river was much higher than it had ever been since I'd lived there—as high, in fact, as it could get without spilling over the edges of the bank. I went onto my porch to make sure I was seeing straight and, as if on cue, the water rose up, up, up—and topped the banks. It came toward the house in a torrent, sweeping up my lawn chairs first. The previous summer I had done some landscaping and put in a gazebo for a friend's wedding, and I watched the water flip it as if it were made of cardboard, and carry it down the river too.

As I was watching, my first thought was, *Why do I keep choosing to live by rivers?* But I already knew: I love water, and rivers especially. I love the sound they make and the reminder they provide, of life passing by. The second thought was, *Well, I'm happy this is happening after my friend's wedding.* The gazebo would live on the same way that magical day does, in my memory.

Friends who live nearby and weren't affected by the flood came over to help me move a few things around, in case water came into the cottage. We tried to move some of the outdoor furniture too, but the water kept rising, and eventually there wasn't anything to do but stand back and watch the river claim the land.

Still, I was calm. Hopeful, even. I knew that if my home and everything inside it was destroyed, I wouldn't be. I would just have to start over. And I knew beyond a shadow of a doubt that I could do that. Not because I'm a superwoman with unerring instincts and limitless capabilities—as should be abundantly clear by this point, I am not. I am tough in some ways, weak in others, and very much a work in progress.

But I'd proved to myself that I already have everything I need in order to reinvent myself. The wellspring I'd drawn on to make my life better is something I'll always have, as long as I live: me. And that means I can weather whatever the universe throws at me.

Full circle

Sometimes what might look to the rest of the world like a repeat or a redo can actually be a whole new experience for the person who's doing it, because you come to it with a whole new attitude and set of goals, and you derive a different sense of meaning from it. That's how it was for me, anyway, when I returned to television after several years' absence.

After I left *Dragons' Den*, I didn't look back. As I may have mentioned several dozen times now, I was way too busy trying to push forward! Then one day about two years ago, I got a call from the show's executive producer, asking if I'd ever consider returning to the show. I was in my car, taking the call on speakerphone as I drove, and I hesitated so long that she asked if I was still there. Her question had caught me off guard. The idea had never occurred to me.

The truth is, I hadn't liked being labelled a "TV personality," but now I was in a different situation. Before, the show had been the most important thing I did, because it was the most visible and it was also my main point of contact with entrepreneurs, who were my passion.

What a difference a few years had made. Now that our one-stop ecosystem to help entrepreneurs succeed was up and running, I was surrounded by entrepreneurs in our accelerators; the fund was flourishing; Venture was on a solid footing. At this point in my life, the show would be an exclamation point, not the main event, and the publicity would be good for the fund—for the entire ecosystem, actually. And hey, it was also an opportunity to make some good business deals. (Yes, the deals are real. One of the biggest misconceptions about the show is that it's fake. At home, you see the eight-minute version of the pitch, but in the studio, a pitch might take an hour while we hash it out. I assure you, what you see isn't scripted.)

So I said yes. Weirdly enough, not long after that, I got a call to do another show, *Under New Management*, where I help people who want to reinvent their lives choose between three potential businesses they could buy. And I said yes to that too, because it truly is right up my alley—it's what I'm doing myself pretty much every day now, between the fund and the accelerators. I now assess every opportunity using this criterion: will it help build the platform? I don't have time for distractions, no matter how enticing.

On my first day back at *Dragons' Den*, on a cool spring morning, I was excited as I walked through the vast set on the tenth floor of the CBC building in downtown Toronto. It felt both familiar and strange to be passing the long craft table loaded with chafing dishes for lunch and bowls of jujubes for cast and crew. Entrepreneurs huddled backstage, rehearsing their pitches like actors.

Among the staff, a lot of faces were the same. Somehow I'd forgotten how many people it takes to make a TV show, and how exceptional this group was. There was a lot of hugging on the way to my little dressing room. And there was my name on the door, as if I'd never left.

But I had, and that made all the difference. The first day I was ever on the *Den*, and for many, many days, months and years thereafter, I was operating on courage. I was afraid—of being revealed as a fraud, of failing, of letting my team and my family down, of being judged and found wanting. Now, I was confident, not because I knew the drill (though that undoubtedly helped) but because, in some important respects, I wasn't the same person I had been when I first started on the show, a decade before.

I was the old and improved version of myself. Settling into the makeup chair, I felt a little defiant. *Well,* I thought, *the world might expect me to be Botoxed to perfection, and cameras definitely won't subtract the weight I've gained, but who cares? I'm sixty, I've had an incredible couple of years, I've beaten the odds, and here I am, with a chance to help reinvent this show that helped me reinvent myself. How lucky is that?*

This time around, I wanted to represent and reinforce the values and beliefs that I had spent the post-flood years cementing: that entrepreneurship is important to the future of our country; that Canada needs more female leaders; that dreaming big and pushing through failure are both possible. You may be thinking, *Oh, come on—it's a reality show, not a pulpit!* You're right, of course: entertainment is an important part of the show's mandate.

But time away, and my own experience as an entrepreneur, made me much more aware that the show matters, too. It really does help people—not just the ones who actually come on TV to pitch their ideas, but also those who are watching at home—find the confidence and courage to reinvent themselves. It's fashionable to sneer at sincerity, as though wanting to make more of yourself is somehow uncool. But to me, there's nothing cooler or more important than trying to be the best you can be. Isn't that why we're here—to find out all we can do, to change and evolve into better people, and to lift others up when we have the chance?

I was thinking about all of this as I headed to the stage on that first day back. The only familiar face was Jim Treliving's. He's the only Dragon who's been with the show from the very beginning; he and I are the sole survivors from those early days. As I looked around the set, it was evident that a lot had changed. Now, I don't have to carry the "successful woman" mantle alone: two of the other Dragons are women. Equal gender representation was unimaginable when I first started. Change is good.

As the doors opened for the first pitch, I had a happy thought: *Hey, I'm starting all over again. Again.*

Caps off

For many of you, some personal version of a flood prompted you to pick up this book: a heartbreaking loss, a divorce, a professional failure, an injustice that upended everything. I hope you are already well on your way to your reinvention and a better life.

If there's one thing I hope the rest of you take away from this book, it's this: don't wait for a flood. You already have all the ingredients you need. Once you figure out what your currency, your core purpose and your context are, you'll be as ready as you'll ever be to make your life better than it is today. My dad always told me that the most powerful thing we have is free agency, and, as in most things, he was right. So use yours. Now, not later. Reinvention requires not just optimism but a sense of urgency.

For me, what provokes that sense of urgency is an understanding of impermanence that has deepened as the years have flown by. Success, like life, doesn't last forever. It's been jarring to watch companies that were stalwarts for decades—Sears, Toys "R" Us—simply vanish. When I was rebuilding Venture, I was acutely aware that there was a good possibility it too might cease to exist. To make it viable again, it had to become something it had never been before. We had to use the company's currency to fashion a new core purpose for it, then work like hell to fulfill that purpose. We might still have failed, and while that would have been devastating, I would at least have felt that we'd fought the good fight and done the very best we could.

That is as good a measure of success as any: that you tried your very best to be all you could be. At the end of the day, your power, your fulfillment, your growth, your evolution and your joy lie in the effort, not in crossing the finish line. Let's face it, to be *all* you can be, you will have to keep on growing, evolving and changing. There really is no finish line. It's a lifelong project.

For many years, I prevented myself from being all I could be because I put limits on how high I dared to reach. I was at an event recently where the speaker, entrepreneur Seth Godin, cleverly illustrated how self-defeating this is. He asked everyone in the room to raise their hands as high as they possibly could. Immediately, hands shot up, like a thousand kindergartners all in urgent need of a bathroom pass. Then he asked the crowd to raise their hands higher. And guess what? Up went the hands. I caught my breath. Every single person in that room was capable of going higher, but hadn't, until they were told to do so. They'd put a cap on their own ability, then proved that they could easily surpass it.

The take-away: aim high, higher than where you are today, knowing that capping your own dreams is a form of self-betrayal. As much as it hurts to be let down by someone else, it is exponentially more painful when the person who sells you short is you, because self-loathing and shame are bound to follow. Furthermore, in the words of Marianne Williamson, "your playing small doesn't serve the world." Don't deny the world the contribution that only you can make. Whether that's being a better parent, or a better executive, or a better artist, or a better teacher, or a better dog walker, or a better CEO, or a better cashier doesn't matter. The world could use better versions of all of us.

If it turns out that you've dreamed the impossible dream—you just don't have the right currency, or the context is all wrong—don't give up on yourself. Come up with another dream, another goal, and go for it. Remember, you can't do *anything*; you have to work with what you have. But you can do *something*. Something that's aligned with your core purpose. Something that uses all of your unique talents, interests and attributes. Something that makes your life better than it is today.

Everything you need for a reinvention is already inside you, just waiting to be tapped. So get going! I can't wait to see what you do next.

Acknowledgements

The days of our lives can become so intermingled that we don't think to pause and reflect on who we are at any moment, much less where we have come from and what we have learned. Most importantly, we don't think enough about all that we could be. But in writing this book, I had no choice but to pause and take stock, and it was painful at times. It is not easy to admit all the mistakes that led me to reinvent myself, yet again. You never know how the world will receive your truth, and yet one of the most important things I have learned is that that should be the least of your concerns. There is energy and freedom to be gained by expressing both your fears and your dreams, regardless of how they are received. In many ways it is exactly what you need to do in order to try to change your path and your future.

This book would not have been possible without the help of many people. People who have been integral to my ability to carry on when things were at their bleakest. And people who encouraged me when things were going well. You need both cheerleaders and unwavering love in your life. I have been fortunate enough to have both, and yet, often, I didn't even know they were there. Thank you to those people who support me, and also to those who challenge or discourage me. All of you have played a role in helping me get to where I am today.

To my family, my North Stars: Garett, Michael, Carley, Marayna, Carter, Colton, Faith, Hailey and Stella. You have put up with so much: my travel, my work, sharing me with strangers, and the countless interruptions to our holidays, life events and family moments. But your love for me, and mine for you, has remained unwavering. We are not perfect, but my love for you is.

To my friends and fans: you are amazing cheerleaders. Your e-mails, cards, letters and messages, especially when I am down, have helped me get back up. I am so grateful for your encouragement to keep going, "as the play, Arlene, must go on." And I love hearing about your own struggles and victories, despite not always being able to answer. You inspire me.

To the team at Venture, both past and present: you are the reason this book exists. Over thirty years, many people have worked with us. Some have gone on to their own great success, some have moved on because the place wasn't for them; all, however, have left a handprint that ultimately strengthened us. And through it all, at the core, there's always been a team who believe in what we are building. I am grateful beyond measure for those who helped build our business and those who helped rebuild it into a different type of organization that matters in a new way. Our reinvention would not have happened without you.

To the folks at HarperCollins, starting with Kate Cassaday, who commissioned this book, and the incomparable Iris Tupholme, who saw it through to the finish line: this is our third book together and I believe it to be our best. Thank you for your commitment to me and to my story, and for all you have done to make this manuscript come to life; and thank you more generally for your commitment to ensuring that stories survive in a world where change is the only constant.

To Katrina Onstad, thank you for your efforts to help frame this book. You listened and cajoled and helped tease from me some stories I wanted to forget but needed to tell. I appreciate all you did to help me on this journey.

And finally, to Kate Fillion: Sometimes you are lucky enough in life to meet a person who "gets" you and then stays with you, through thick and thin, and through all of your reinventions. Kate, that is you. You were there when I needed you most to be there. We pick up where we leave off. You understood my journey because you've been a part of it and such a dear, dear friend. It's not lost on me that we reinvented my book on reinvention, and that we did it together. Without you, this book would not be as deeply and personally meaningful. Without you, the lessons I had to share would not be communicated as clearly. And without you, I would not have recognized that I am indeed now finally an entrepreneur. Thank you is not enough. We will cycle together when we can, but we will journey through life together always as friends. No matter the rising waters.